Illumination

The Loving Light Books Series

Also by Liane Rich

Loving Light

Book 14

Illumination

Liane Rich

The information contained in this book is not intended as a substitute for professional medical advice. Neither the publisher nor the author is engaged in rendering professional advice to the reader. The remedies and suggestions in this book should not be taken, or construed, as standard medical diagnosis, prescription or treatment. For any medical issue or illness consult a qualified physician.

Loving Light Books
Original Copyright © 1994
Copyright © 2010 Liane

ISBN 13: 978-1-878480-14-9
ISBN 10: 1-878480-14-6

Loving Light Books:
www.lovinglightbooks.com

Also Available at:
Amazon: www.amazon.com
Barnes & Noble: www.barnesandnoble.com

for Jim

The information in this series is not necessarily meant to be taken literally. It is meant to *shift* your consciousness....

Foreword

Anyone immersed in the vast body of new metaphysical knowledge is aware of the virtual symphony of voices from channeled sources throughout the world – inspirational voices that may be artistic, poetic, philosophical, religious, or scientific. And now, out of these myriad New Age voices, comes a series of books by God, channeled through Liane, revealing the frank truth in all its glory and wonder, telling us how to cleanse our bodies, gain access to our subconscious minds, clear our other selves and march back to who we are – God.

In God's books you will be introduced to a loving, powerful, gripping, exciting, and often humorous voice that reaches out and speaks ever so personally to the individual reader. As the reader's interest deepens, invariably an intimate relationship to this voice develops. It is a relationship that lasts forever, and I am quite certain I do mean forever.

Here is an accelerated program, a no-holds-barred course, where God guides us and loves us, and as needs be recommends books to us and even a movie or musical piece along the way. He (She) enters our lives and sees through our eyes, seeming to enjoy the ride as He guides us back to US, back to ALL. Here is a voice that is playful and informative, that is humorous and serious, that is gentle and powerfully divine. It is a voice that knows no barriers or restrictions, a straightforward and honest voice that caresses us when we need the warmth and pushes us when we are immobilized.

In today's New Age literature there is an avalanche of information from magnificent beings of light, information that possesses us and compels us to look at our fears and express our love. In this series of books by God, you will find truly powerful methods for making this transition from toxicity to purity, from density to light, from fear to love, and from the delusion of death to the awakening to full life. You will experience in these books the love and the power of God for it is your love to express and your power to behold. Rarely will you see more lucid steps for transformation. Read these beautiful words and rejoice in our period of awakening, our return to Home.

John Farrell, PhD., LCSW. – Psychologist, Clinical Social Worker, Senior Clinician Psychiatric Emergency Services, U.C. Davis Medical Center, Sacramento. John is also a retired Professor – California State University, Sacramento, in Health Sciences and Psychology.

Illumination

Introduction

You will begin to see how you are God when you begin to see how you shine. You will begin to see how all are God by looking at how they shine. You are all emanating light. You are all part of light and you are illuminating to the extent that you have arisen. You can only shine as brightly as you can see. You can shine as brightly as you are clear in your intent. Your intent must be pure in that your intent must be love. When your intent is love, your vibration speeds up and you are able to love. Love emits light for all to see. This is also how you draw greater light to you. Your intent is your biggest draw. If your intent is pure, your light is pure in its source and therefore extremely "brilliant." If your intent is not based in love, you will find that your light may flicker and die out and you must again reignite it.

It is well known that man has sought to evolve from the beginning of time. His evolution has been slow but the results can be traced all through history. You are now making your greatest leap in evolution. This leap is beyond historical or traditional value. This leap is a giant step into the "spirit" of God. You are becoming spirit minded and God centered. You are growing in God as God grows in you. You are becoming God by allowing God to become you. You are expanding your own awareness to the extent that you can draw strength from your own energy, your own source. You will no longer require love from another to sustain your true nature which is love. You will be allowed by your own evolution to sustain and nurture your own self, and you will no longer feel the need to seek love from others.

This will create a most amazing relationship between those you choose to have regard for. You will find that you no longer *need* to receive nurturing or caring or understanding from others. The interesting thing will be that you are so full of your own nurturing and caring and understanding that you will literally emanate forth nurturing and caring and understanding. It will become so full in you that it overflows into your daily life and onto your world. Think how grand this will be, to be so full of caring and comforting and nurturing that you never feel drained, you only feel "full" of love to give to everyone and everything.

Now; we all know in this class how love cannot really be given, as it is not a possession that one places in someone else's care. It is not like the emotions that can so easily be attached to the partner in a relationship and then unattached when you are finished with that particular partner. Love does not attach and love does not hold on to. Love flows constantly and so you may guide your love in certain directions as you would guide a light. Love is a light!

Love is your light and you may shine your light in any direction you choose.

Love emanates from you as a light would emanate from a giant searchlight. The beam goes forth and casts its brilliance on whatever and whoever it touches. This is the light of love. This is the brilliance of illumination. When you begin to have pure intent, your love light will be so big it will overwhelm and override everything else. No need or desire will get in the way of your becoming total light. All desires will take a back seat, and the more light you emanate the more you dissolve your own fears which are based in darkness. The light of your intent will literally wipe away your fears.

You are moving into a most glorious time for yourselves and I do enjoy riding with you. You are allowing God to work through matter simply by allowing it. You are *allowing* God to become you simply by *allowing* it. You are allowing God to heal humanity simply by allowing it. You are the light and the love, and you may nurture and care for all humanity simply by caring enough for you to heal you and love you. You are moving from intent to harm you and punish you for past sins into intent to love you and care for you no matter what you have done. When you have accomplished this you will have healed the world; your world. And everywhere you look you will see your light and your love instead of your darkness and your fear.

You have come a long way and you are just now beginning to open up your heart and love you. Congratulations! Once you move into your love center you will be free of self-punishment, judgment and guilt. You will be in a state of grace which is embodied in trust and faith. Nothing, absolutely nothing, can harm you when you believe in love. Because, when you believe in love, nothing else exists for you. You are home!

❧

*W*hen you come to know God you will have within you the ability to love all. God is love and God has this ability to shine his light on absolutely anyone and everyone. It will not matter what type the personality is or how the personality has acted or what the personality believes. God loves all. So, as you begin to fall in sync with your own God-self you will find it difficult to find anything wrong with anyone. You will be so attuned to looking for the good that you will find it impossible to see the bad. Bad will begin to disappear in your world and you will no longer know that it even exists for others. It simply will no longer have anything to do with you nor will it have any power over you. You will become good and everyone else will become good also.

As you begin to move into this new perspective, you will begin to know that you are moving into love. Love does not judge and love does not condemn. Love simply allows and accepts and flows. It is not the type of love that you have been taught exists. Love is actually quite forgiving, in that it never judges to begin with so everything is automatically forgiven. In the eyes of love there are no sins and there are no sinners. In the eyes of love there is only light, beautiful magnificent light. You are beginning to move into this light now. As you do, I wish you to remember that you still carry certain shadows of fear that will be dissolved by the light. The shadows will first be exposed when the light of truth hits them and then you will be allowed to face them and release them. This is often a tough part of transformation for you. You do not like having to face your buried garbage, but please allow this process and know that you will be better for it.

You are now beginning to acquire a deep feeling of movement in a new direction. You may feel as though you have succeeded to a new level of awareness, or you may simply feel like you are finally beginning to see a light at the end of a very long tunnel. However you feel is how you are now. Do not mistrust your feelings. I know that often you begin to feel like you are finally reaching a level of peace only to be hit again with another fear. This is a gradual rise whereby you will increase your light source while you clean out your debris. As your light source increases, your debris leaving you increases. This may become quite confusing for you. You are actually moving and vibrating so rapidly that you are stirring up all the old garbage that you carry, and it brings you down and even exhausts you as it leaves. This is all part of this process! Do not be upset. This is garbage leaving and being seen as it goes. You cannot help but see it because your light is exposing it.

As you move to greater levels of awareness, your garbage will dwindle and you will simply work with a minimum of maintenance to continue your releasing. Once the basic concepts of your nature, which have been dysfunctional for you, are released you will begin to simply siphon off any debris that is still liquid and not yet hardened into basic concepts. You will find that as these basic concepts begin to dissolve you will feel much better. These concepts or ideas are not wrong; they are simply outdated and no longer true. You will find that as you release these concepts your life will begin to shift dramatically. You will be much freer in your thinking and in your living. As you free up these areas you will also free up your spirit. The freer your spirit becomes, the more able to assist you spirit is. You are moving into spirit now and you are no longer going to fear love/God/self. You are going to trust love/God/self. You are love/God/self.

∂⁄⁄∕

You will begin to understand light when you let go of darkness. In order to know and to understand illumination you must experience being light. Once you have experienced being light you will never again crave darkness. There is a sense of well-being that cannot be duplicated and this sense of well-being comes only from living in the light. When awareness and clarity arrive, I assure you that you will most enjoy the effects. As you learn to live within the light and to know clarity, you will begin to know God and to sense true love and compassion for everyone and everything. This compassion will be pure, in that you will have nurtured yourself to the extent that the overflow will reach out to others. When you live in the light you will feel nothing but love. True love is bliss and bliss flows forth from true love. As you reach this state you will feel very good indeed.

Once you have begun to allow light to take over, you will be most surprised at your own ability to enjoy love and to spread love. You will find it most difficult to hide your feeling of bliss and you will find it most difficult to stop or even slow down your love flow. The light of your love will be so bright that many will be drawn to you. You will find that not only are they drawn they are also repelled. Some still fear the light and do not wish to expose their own pain to the light. This creates anxiety for them and they find it necessary to stay hidden in fear until they feel safe enough to face fear. As you encounter those who wish to stay hidden, I wish to remind you to allow everyone to evolve at their own rate and not project your reality and your truth on them. Allow everyone to be who they are and you will be allowing you to be who you are.

Once you achieve a state of well-being through your ascension into light, you still have a long way to go. If you begin to make a big deal about being in the light, you will get stuck and not flow with the rest of the plan. Yes! There is more, and arriving in the light does not give you total ascension. There are always higher levels of awareness and greater love. So, don't get too carried away with your celebrating, and don't convince the others to follow you when you don't even know where you are going. You will find that you are not only 'not' aware of where you are going, you actually have no idea how you really got to the light in the first place. You think it may be this or may be that, but you are not certain. When you are certain and when you know all there is to know you will come from God. Until then you are coming from man.

So, use your ascension wisely. Do not boast and do not push at others to try it. Let everyone do their own thing at their own speed. You have done well to arrive but you are only on the loading dock and your journey is just beginning. Your ship has just pulled in but you have not yet sailed.

You will wish to know that you do not arrive in the light alone. You may feel alone for awhile but you will not be alone for long. As you clear your own sense of well-being, you will draw those to you who have also cleared and are walking in the light. The greatest benefit of being in the light is seeing with clarity. When you live in the dark everything is dark and you not only cannot see in front of you, you also cannot see behind you. In the light you have both foresight and hindsight. You know where you are going and you know where you have been.

It is also easier to stumble and fall in the dark. In the light you clearly see obstacles and so you can go around them instead of crashing head on with them. Fewer collisions are created and less scar tissue. This also means no pain, as no one is butting their heads or tripping over one another. It's a much better way to live with less fighting and a great deal more peace. It is much more conducive to your spirit, and a happy spirit can soar.

So, as you begin to move into the light you will let go of your old need to go head-to-head with others. You will no longer need to prove to anyone how wise you are or how much credibility you carry. You will be feeding yourself all the love and acceptance and appreciation you could possibly need, so why try to get it from another. You are moving into a place that will be very, very "bright." You will smile, you will dance, you will sing in your heart. This lightness comes from within. It comes from letting go of the pain and confusion that you are now releasing and it comes to show you how to move to the next level.

The lightness of illumination is all that you will ever want from where you now stand, but believe me when I say "there is more." There are wonders to behold that are much greater than you can imagine. Do not limit your imagination to simply illumination. Go on to the totality of "all that is" and you will be touching God. You will find that you do not touch God simply by rising up out of the grunge of darkness. You touch God by learning who you are. You will very much enjoy this phase of your training, but for now we will stick with where you are, which is moving from darkness into light. Welcome to the doorway. You are doing just fine and you deserve a pat on the back. Please give yourself one right now.

❧

You once began to rise up and come awake out of a desire to return to your natural state. At that time you became aware that you no longer had control over you. The magnetic pull of darkness had sucked you in and you were unable to allow yourselves the necessary power surge to rise up out of the material plane. Now you are beginning to loosen your grip on your belief *in* this plane and that is enough to allow you to begin to leave. You were never meant to be stuck. You got so carried away with your fun and excitement that you forgot that you are "just passing through." You do not belong to this world of heaviness. You do belong in lightness and love and fun and joy and frivolity. You belong in a place that is totally opposite of what you now see and the way home is now being paved.

Do you remember what it feels like to have an entire day with nothing but joy and bliss – no questions, no problems, no stress, no sadness, no disruptions, no interruptions, nothing but joy and bliss for an entire day – no questioning or searching for answers because you already know all that is necessary, no searching for peace as you already have peace and no hopes for tomorrow as today is so joyful that tomorrow will automatically be the same? This is where you ultimately belong. This is how you ultimately believe and exist.

The only problem now is how to get you back to your true existence. That is why I write these books for you. You are returning to you after a long journey to the opposite side of creation and you will learn to transform into your old nature simply by not struggling. It is as though you are in thick, thick mud and the more you struggle, the deeper into the mud you sink. This is why I ask you to stay calm. I am not trying to pacify you for my own sake; I am trying to get you to stop kicking and flailing so you do not sink deeper and drown in the mud.

You must come to a point of realization that will allow you to stay calm and stop getting excited. This will allow you to float free of the suction that is being created by all your struggling. When you begin to let go of your fear of going under you will calm down enough to be released from this pull. You are not drowning in mud. You only believe that you are because you came into an evolutionary world that shows you what you believe and not what is true. This is the *key* to this world. It is ruled by thought and belief. If you want out, change how you think and what you believe.

You will find that you are the most amazing beings in that you have the ability to *form* your own choice of realities. This is one of the reasons you first came to play in the material realms. Here you are allowed to be who you think you are and escape who you really are. You thought this would be great fun! In the beginning it was. Now you have forgotten that you can change form simply by changing your mind about who you wish to be. You have lost your magic and your beauty by *believing* that only certain shapes and certain sizes are magical and beautiful. You are *all* magical and beautiful; you just chose to forget for a while. Now you are coming awake and you will remember. You will begin to see how beautiful you are and you will begin to feel your magic. You are spirit! You are wondrous to behold and, once we get you up out of the mud, you will see how you got stuck and you will know how not to do it again. Unless, of course, you wish to go unconscious again – a good black out you might call it.

So now you are a being of light and you are having this blissful, joyous day, and you do not wish to be alone so you start pushing at another to join you in your joy. What happens? The others are busy struggling and will not wish to be pulled up into your world. Your world is for you so don't be upset if, after you create your heaven on earth, no one believes you. You will find that each individual creates from his or her own imagination. Heaven for one is not heaven for another. Just as your hell may appear to be good to another, so your heaven may appear to be awful to another.

Each individual is different and that brings us to colors and differences. You have a very difficult time accepting differences and the idea that everyone should be accepted for themselves and allowed to do their own thing. This is okay. You will learn, as you rise above the mud level, that you really can't see much or know much when you are kicking and flailing in thick mud. So your opinion really has as much authority as the opinion of a rock. Actually a rock might have a clearer point of perspective than you do, but you get the idea.

So; until you get up out of the mud I want you to stay out of the opinion business, and by all means stay calm. Use your new found sense of calm and your new found guidance to help you stay in the light and away from the ignorance of darkness. After all, you are tired of playing in the dark and you wish to return to the light. This is a very good time to move into the light as this is the time of the light. Light is pouring forth and light is surrounding this plane now. Why do you think you are all so jittery? The jig is up! Your game is busted! The lie is dying! The light is shining down into the darkness and exposing it for what it is. It is only an illusion. It is a trick. It is not true.

You will find that as you move forward into the light, the most magical experiences will begin to occur. You will begin to see how the darkness was just a pretend situation to see how far you would go into the illusion. You will see that it is not at all real and there is no need to expose yourself to this unreality. You will find that, as you begin to unravel this part of yourself, you will see how your beliefs from the past are what drive you into your future. Your past does not exist and your future does not exist. You are simply playing a big game and the game is coming to an end.

❧

You are the most magnificent when you are light. You have the ability to shine and to stay in love. You are one of the most special of beings as you are the host of God. You are the one who cares for and nurtures God. In caring for and nurturing you, you are nurturing and caring for God – the light. As you learn to discover greater and greater parts of your own beingness you will be discovering God. You will uncover the God that is in you and has always been in you. You will discover that you are not only God; you are also "all that is." You are part of every living and nonliving thing and you are part of the great beingness that is centered in this universe. You are part of a collective soul energy that has a purpose. The purpose of this soul energy is to rise up and heal. The purpose of the healing is to accelerate beyond this dimension.

As you begin to show signs of awakening, you will begin to hope for greater opportunity to rise higher and higher in this domain. This will allow you the chance to heal and to become all that you can be. As you heal, you *release* disease and toxins and poisons and pain and struggle. You become free and you begin to rise up out of darkness and show some signs of willingness in completing your task. You each have a purpose for being here and you will soon wake up to that purpose. Once you know your purpose you will be fulfilling your own dreams, because you will be completing your lifespan through purpose rather than through necessity. You are beginning to see how you are drawn to certain areas or even pushed into certain areas (sometimes pull feels like push). As you move into your appointed area, you will begin to feel at home and "right." This type of right is more like a good fit or fitting right in. This is how you will know your right place. It will feel right.

So, as you begin to awaken and your purpose becomes known, I wish you to remember that your purpose was chosen long before you came here and your purpose is your way of *expressing* you. Love is expressed through you and all around you. Your purpose is your life.

You will find that your purpose is often connected to joy and bliss and peace. Find your purpose and you will be in joy and love and peace, or find joy and love and peace and you will be in your purpose. You are not meant to suffer and toil and struggle. You are meant to rise up and know that you are God and you are love and loved. You are the magnificent being of light. You are hooked up to it. You are part of it. You are it. Stop pretending that you are not part of everyone and everything else, for you are. You are this giant being who has grown to such great proportions that he no longer recognizes parts of himself. You are wondrous in your ability to go unconscious and forget. Now you are going to see how well you remember and reconnect.

Hold on for the ride of your life. Time is spinning out of control and you are spinning as fast as you have in a very long time. You are moving forward in a very impressive leap and you will feel this leap within your heart. Your heart is the center of all activity that is connecting you to the giant soul of being. You are beginning to truly "be" for the first time. To "be" is to rise above time and to surrender to God. Simply be my children. Do not struggle. Let it all "be."

You will begin to feel as though you have two selves. You will find that when you are afraid you have mistrust and insecurity. When you are love you have trust and faith and you are most secure. As you begin to operate from love, your other self will gradually fade away. You will forget what it is like to have fear and mistrust and lack of faith. You will begin to feel safe no matter where you are and no matter what you are doing. Most of you have created a realm of safety around you. You feel safe in your own home and in your own territory so to speak. As you evolve, your territory becomes all of creation and you begin to feel safe in all of creation.

Safety comes from feelings of trust and love and knowingness. As you move into these realms, I wish you to remember that you are free when you are love. You need not feel that you must control you or control anyone else. You are free and you are safe to be you. You are in a state of true freedom, as it is a freedom of restraint against the movement of spirit within you. You have just begun the process of setting you free and knowing that you can do absolutely anything you wish; no more rules and no more limiting thoughts that say, "You are bad, you are wrong, you are stupid." You will begin to know your own glory and you will begin to leave you alone and stop being so hard on yourself. If you see how you are hard on others, it is nothing compared to how hard you are on you.

You will find that as you begin to set you free you will still find faults and try to stop yourself from soaring to new heights. This is part of the shift. It is the residue left by fear and it will take a little time to clear it away. As you begin this shift from dark to light, you will begin to know how you are not such a bad person. As a matter of fact you will actually begin to like yourself. This is not arrogance, it is simply a great appreciation of the self, and we all know in this class that with appreciation comes more of the same. So, learn to love yourself and appreciate yourself and stop putting yourself down. It is time to rise up and shine and show yourself off for yourself. Show you what you can do. Perform for you and stop performing for everyone else. Let you be in love with you, and let you dress up for you and speak nice words for you and take special care of you. Treat you as you would treat someone you just fell head over heels in love with. Romance you and show you how loving you can be.

This is your lesson for today. I wish you to be very, very attentive to you. You deserve some love in your life. Buy you flowers and take you to a movie, and really learn about who you are and what you like and how you were raised, just as you would with a real date. Talk to you, get to know you. You make a very nice friend and a truly wonderful lover. You are special and you are one of a kind. Get to know you as I do. Love you as I do. Let yourself be special and let yourself know that you are never alone for you always have you.

As you begin to know how you are indeed connected to the light, you will begin to know how you are love. It is love that is the flow of life. It is love that creates all life and it is love that is the balance necessary for creation. Love is all that truly exists and love is all that ever was. When you begin to uncover your love light, you will begin to feel love as an energy center. You will begin to know that love flows through you just as blood flows through your veins. Love is the brightest, most responsive energy as it may penetrate as well as absorb. It is both male and female in its essence. It is neither given nor is it taken. It simply exists at a very high vibration and is felt the higher you evolve.

It is not that love is so much in your life as it *is* your life. You are love, which is life, and you shut down living so love got shut out too. So, how do we get you to turn on your love light? Simply by asking you to love you. When you begin to love and accept you, you will be loving and accepting love. You – the essence of you is love. So all that is required for you to become what you already are is for you to learn to accept what you already are.

You are beginning to accept you now, and with acceptance will come true understanding and even appreciation of all that you are. This will include past lives and their purpose as well as this life and its purpose. Bless your life and know that it is all for a purpose. Know that you are evolving and each time you hurt yourself you are allowed to reach a higher choice. You need not complete any cycle that was agreed upon for karmic reasons. You may let go of all belief that you owe anyone for your karmic debts. You have played this game of cause and effect into the ground and now you can let go. You need never return for lessons once you begin to wake up and realize it is all a big game. No one has the responsibility to return and reincarnate simply to save this planet. This planet will do just fine with or without you, and you may find that it evolves much quicker once you evolve enough to raise yourself above it.

You are moving into very confusing times, in that most of those you see will begin to panic over what they see. It will create havoc and many will resist rising because they are stuck to and in fear. It is important at this time to allow them their own path. You are creating your new world by your new belief system. As you create your new world you may not invite others into it. It is yours. It is a way of viewing reality and it is not possible to bring another into your reality. They must have a like reality in order to see common ground and share your enthusiasm. This is done by them creating their own reality and it matching yours.

Other than this, you are pretty much on your own in your newly created heaven. You may, however, create friends who see what you see, by drawing to you like minded people. This allows you to view realities and make similar observations. You never create exactly the same reality until you rise up out of the reality business. This will occur when you have gone beyond creation and you no longer play in these realms. For now, however, we will speak to you from where you are.

You are beginning to move into a new area of creation that I will call ascended awareness. In your state of ascended awareness, you will sit and observe your world with a whole new perspective. As you observe, you will begin to appreciate all that you have created simply by switching your focus from bad to good or from wrong to right.

When you begin to allow everyone (even you) to be good and right, you will create an entirely new view of your world. Everything in your world will shift when you shift. This is because you are the projector not the projection. You learn to focus and get a clear picture and then you focus outward and – voilà! A picture is formed. You may use this picture anyway you want. The picture is yours. It is your inner created reality focused outward onto nothing. Space is nothing until it is intercepted with light or dark. So, here we have you projecting your newly created reality out onto nothingness and turning that nothingness into your perspective or your point of view. If your perspective involves love you create an outer picture of love. If your perspective involves fear you create an outer projection of fear.

An outer world is created from within. Do you see love and understanding or do you see fear and chaos? It is all coming from the inner realms. All shifts take place within and are vibrated out. You send signals and you don't know that you do. You attract what you are to you by sending out a signal that says, "This is what I am. Who is looking for this?" You are a walking advertisement for your own inner turmoil and chaos or peace and love. You may decide to slow down the signals that you send, by simply shutting down your *search* for like-minded individuals until you have adjusted your own perspective enough to know what you are advertising. You always advertise you, but do you know you?

You are never meant to be in danger. When you walk in danger you are walking in fear. Most of you have created realities filled with excitement and adventure. If you love excitement and adventure, you will see yourself in this movie role. You each project what you crave and you each control your own pattern of existence. If you are tired of excitement, I suggest you begin to look at your distaste towards calm. What you call boring may be what you really want, but you got so hooked into excitement and chaos that you now create it wherever you go. If things get too calm you begin to feel anxious and so you start an argument, or you purposely begin to push someone else's buttons to get your juices flowing so you can feel alive and excited. You are no longer feeling this great need for thrill and that is why you are beginning to search for peace and calm.

When you become more aware of how you stir things up to suit your purpose (which is excitement) you will begin to know how you really do create your reality and all that occurs in it. You will begin to see how you actually like to live on the edge of uncertainty as it allows you the stimulation you so desperately desire. If you are uncertain of your position at work, or in a relationship, it adds intrigue and suspense and even challenge. When things get boring you feel that your life is over and you are old and useless. Nothing seems important because your zing is not flying, and so you want to create something important to make you *feel* important.

The unfortunate thing is that most of you create anger and frustration and boredom out of peace. You have time on your hands, and nothing is happening so you get impatient and begin to stir the soup because you think it will cook faster if you do. Leave it alone. Learn to enjoy boredom at least as much as you do excitement. Learn to allow everything to unfold in its own time. Allow God to deliver your good without kicking and screaming that you are "in need now." God knows what you need and it is not what you think it is. Be still, be quiet and allow God to deliver.

You are now in a place of service to God. You may assist God simply by being patient and watching what is unfolding before you. Do not judge, do not criticize, simply watch. Sit peacefully and know that all good is unfolding. All are doing exactly what is necessary to show you what you need to see. Yes! This show is for you. If you see it, it is for you. It is you creating what you are. When you begin to allow God to create for you, you allow for a shift in what is being created. Allow God to take over and he will advertise God and not identity. You will find that the projections God will send out will be much different than what the average ego identity sends out. Why? God does not need, so God does not fear not getting. Let God take over. Move over and get out of the driver's seat. Give control over to God. Let God drive for awhile.

I know you fear not knowing where you are going, but God has a direct route to heaven. He knows it very well. Do you? He has this ability to transcend time and space. Do you? Allow God to drive and you take a passenger seat. Do this in your job, in your life, in your health, in your play, in your reality. Do not worry about tomorrow for God is in charge. Do not worry about your love life for God is in charge. Do not worry about the fate of the world for God is in charge. Trust God. Give it over to God. Know that God loves you and is taking real good care of you.

God is being born in you and you get to say how far, how fast and how strong he may become. Give that right to control over to God and allow him to come in strong. You only allow God to work within you to a certain degree and now it is time to shift into gear and allow God to do his thing. No, you need not know what God's thing is. Your job is to trust. God's job is to be God. You allow room for trust and God will do the rest. In every situation I wish you to simply give up and turn it over to God. This will allow you to walk with God by your side and it will allow you to know what God has in store for you. Trust

God! Know what God knows by allowing him to take over your life. Let God be you by letting God take over you.

You are now moving into a phase of total acceptance. With acceptance of God comes acceptance of you. You get a double win when you take in God. You get God, you get you and you learn to accept all in one shot. Not bad for a day's work. You will no longer find it necessary to be in charge once you accept that God can do a much better job. You have done well with your lessons and they have brought you to this point in time. Release what you think you own to God. Give up you to God. Love God enough to ask God to take you back. You came from God and the whole idea is to return to God. Feel it! Know it! Live it!

Live in God. Let God be in charge. Allow God to do it for you, to say it for you and to allow you the freedom to truly live. You have no idea what living is really about. You think you do, but you do not. God will show you the beauty you have always wanted. God will show you the love you so desperately search for. It is all *in* God. God holds life in his hands. God holds all truths and all secrets and all that will create heaven on earth. Many have worked at ascending from the ego identity but it does not work. Ascension comes with God. God is part of you and he is the part that rises up. Allow God to take control, and allow God to take you out of the mud and grunge that you so desperately cling to.

You think things are one way, but they are not. You do not know the full picture. You may flounder and wander and try to find your way for many more lifetimes, or you may give up to God, and simply forget about leading and forget about finding your way and allow God to do it for you. You are moving into a state of trust that will allow you to give up to God. This choice will be yours as all choices are.

⚜

You do remember how to activate God and you do remember how to allow God in. It will all come back to you and you will come back to God. When you do not wish to be God you simply shut off and allow your ability "to know" to stop. When you want to wake up and remember; you simply allow your ability "to know" to open and start. It is okay to shut it off and it is okay to turn it on. You can do whatever you want when you want. It is your choice and it is your will. As you begin "to know" once again, you will begin to accept how you are made up of many things. Everything that exists is connected to you and, therefore, part of you. You are part of everything and you are part of God.

As you begin to see how you are part of God, you will begin to see how you no longer wish to be separate from God. So now you wish to reintegrate and it seems next to impossible to once again work for God and allow God in. This will become easier as time passes and your desire to grow back towards God increases. The desire to return is all that is necessary to set you in motion. The desire to return is now in you and you will automatically be drawn to what you desire, just as you are drawn by other desires. If your desire to see justice handed down is strong, you will create a system of realities based on justice and centered around right and wrong. If your desire is to see everyone happy and pain-free, you will create a system of realities that respond to this particular desire. Desire plays an important role and always has.

As you learn to control your desires, you will learn to control your creations. As you learn to switch from desiring another's retribution to asking total love and peace for others, you will be creating a reality in which everyone is good and successful and no one is bad and punished. This type of reality is based on true forgiveness and acceptance. This type of reality has let go of the need for revenge and punishment. This type of reality can be most enlightening and most enjoyable.

Is there someone you are holding a grudge against? Is there someone you are upset with? Hope for only love and peace for this individual. Do not wish for penance for his or her sins or you create a reality filled with justice and injustice. Justice is not a viable option. Justice does not work in God's world, for in God's world all is equal and no show of equality is necessary. When you wish for the downfall of another, be it your enemy or a "bad person" in the news, you are wishing for your own downfall. You are connected to "all" and when you hope for someone else to get back "what they deserve" you are hoping for "an eye for an eye." When you hope for that same individual to be safe and in love you are hoping for healing. You get the healing! Whatever you ask for "for yourself" is what you will ask for "for others." If you secretly believe that you deserve to be punished you will wish for punishment for another. If you truly understand how you are God you will ask forgiveness and love for another and, in that process, you will *receive* forgiveness and love from your own self.

Whatever you give out, you give directly to yourself. Your energy runs through you, it does not run over to the other person and create illness in their body. Your thoughts make you ill; they do not run over to your neighbor and make him or her ill. You are killing you with your hatred and anger, just as surely as you might go crazy and shoot another out of hatred and anger. It takes a great deal of anger to kill, and you can see how full of anger you are by looking at how badly you want others to get what they deserve for what they have done in the way of crime or immorality. When you want others to be punished, it is a dipstick to show you how badly you want punishment and how deep this desire goes. Let go of such desires and begin to love yourself. Your mirror is always there to show you who you really are and how you really feel towards you. Look at how you feel towards others and you will know how you feel regarding your own self.

As you begin to discover all parts of you, you will begin to want to free all parts in order to know God. God cannot enter where God is not wanted. If you cannot allow love and acceptance, you cannot allow God, for love and acceptance are God. You will find that as you turn more and more towards God, you will be loving and accepting all parts of you and this is what you have been waiting for your entire life. Love you and accept you. You will see how you have kept love and acceptance at a distance your entire life. Watch your dipstick and you will know how well you are accepting and loving you by how well you are loving and accepting others.

꧁꧂

*A*s you begin to know how you are chasing God away, you will begin to see how your acceptance of God is your acceptance of yourself as well as your acceptance of "all that is". When you begin to accept "all that is", you allow it to become part of your reality. This in turn allows you to become part of "all that is". If you want to become God you simply accept God. If you want to become you, you simply accept you, and if you want to become peace you simply accept peace. Yours is a path of acceptance and allowing all to flow.

You do not receive peace by looking out your window and assuming the worst. If you see two individuals fighting and shooting it out it has nothing to do with you and your peace. If you want peace, you will simply look upon this situation and know that it is simply a struggle that was agreed upon in order to learn a lesson. You do not go to a boxing match that was set up and arranged and begin to scream, "Oh my God they're killing each other.

Stop this madness." Madness and violence are what you say they are. If the baby is flailing and he is kicking and crying, and you get too close, you are going to get hit or kicked. Does this make the baby an attacker, or did this simply show you how silly it is to interfere when a baby is kicking and screaming.

Many of you have never really matured and you are still kicking and screaming. Get out of the way if you do not wish to get hit. Move if someone is striking out at you, and you will be avoiding a hit that would have been given to whoever was there. Most of your fights and arguments have nothing to do with you or another. They have to do with you being where you can get hit or you getting involved when it is not necessary.

Peace will bring you to this awareness. You will no longer be in a position to be hurt, as you will no longer desire pain in order to feel alive. You will begin to allow others to say what they wish to and to express their feelings however they wish to. You may call this violence and awfulness and horrific behavior, or you might want to calm down and observe. An observer will notice two individuals acting out emotions. An antagonist or glory seeker or enthusiastic participant will see violence and danger and bizarre behavior. You get to name everything and this will tell you how you are seeing your reality. If you glorify and horrify, you are an excitable individual. If you simply observe as you would with two children playing with toy guns, you are learning the way of peace.

I know that you have been taught to save others, and to interfere, and to take charge, and even to step in front of another to take the hit for them. This is all up to you and a matter of choice. If you wish to hold on to the old way of thinking it is your free will choice. If you wish to move into peace, I suggest you give up trying to be Superman, and begin to believe that "there is no injustice" so you need not fight for justice.

$\approx$

As you return to God you will begin to feel as though you had never left. You will be free to think good thoughts and to be positive regarding your life and your future. You are moving from a life of unknown despair into a life of promise and hope. You will find that you not only love life, you will love all aspects of your own self. You will begin to enjoy all that is presented to you and you will begin to know how you are truly joyful. You will exhibit ways of returning to God that will be an example for others to follow. This is how you lead. You lead simply by being love and watching to see who else wishes to be love. You do not recruit others to join you in your cause. You simply allow all to follow in your footsteps and you allow all to be who they request to be.

As you begin to open to love you will find that you no longer feel the need to criticize nor to correct. This will become sheer nonsense, as you will know that there are many truths and many realities, and who are you to judge or to tell someone how to live their life. When you impose your restrictions on another you are imposing your will on another. When you fight to change things you are pushing your ideas and your way of thinking on others. Your way is only your way, and I wish you to remember that when you open to God you open to "all that is," not just your way but "all ways."

You are not so very smart when you begin to push at another. The reason you push is a desire to change what you are seeing. This is not being an observer; this is being a changer and a manipulator. You wish to be God and know God. You will know God by allowing everyone to be who they wish to be. You be you if you can, and allow them to be themselves. You are not here to control even though you think you are. You are here to love and to accept and to know. This does not mean knowing only one way. This does mean knowing all.

You are moving into a phase which will be difficult for you. It is called "change." Not change thy neighbor or change thy world, but change thyself. You must be willing to change and let go of this incessant need to control. Stop controlling. Stop telling everyone how to live. Stop creating holes in the spirit by saying how incorrect things are. You are leaving out big chunks of God that you obviously know nothing about. How can you tell another that he or she is incorrect when you know less than two percent of the whole that is waiting to be discovered? You know next to nothing, and yet you stand and shout about injustice and crime and the awfulness of this situation or that situation. Stop tagging everything as awful or incorrect. Everything is perfect. That person you think is awful is doing exactly what he was meant to do, and that jerk at the office is more correct in his or her behavior than you can ever know. You have such limited vision that you must stop demanding attention by pretending that your answers are better than someone else's answers. This gets you into limited viewpoints and I wish you to be unlimited in thought and action.

When you begin to know how you are pushing at everyone to see things your way, you will begin to see how you are pushing away the very essence that is God. God is all sides of everything, all points of view and all positions. You cannot accept one point of view or one way of doing something and expect to accept God. To accept God you must first accept that you know so very little that it causes you to reject all that you do not know. At this point, all that you do not know is the majority of "all that is." When you get to a point where you can accept "all that is," you will be accepting God. You will be "open" to acceptance.

So; how close to God are you? How are you doing in your acceptance? Have you gotten beyond pushing your reality at everyone else, or do you still insist that your way is better than another's? You will learn as you go that your way is simply how you feel right now and tomorrow you may change how you feel regarding any one position you now hold. Let go of all positions. Let go of everything. Hold nothing and know nothing. I want no facts, no opinions. I want "open," empty minds to fill with pure wisdom that will flow through and not settled in. Stay calm and know that your neighbor is God and just as valid as you. He or she is also your reflection, if you tag he or she a jerk – guess who you are really tagging a jerk? Let it all go. There is never ever a need to try to push at or change anyone. Simply be and let be. Exist and allow to exist. You are dealing directly with you. All fights are fights with you. All abuse is with yourself. You are both sides playing against itself. Stop, look, listen. It is only you....

❧

You will begin to become aware of your thoughts regarding your own personality and how you see yourself, by becoming aware of your thoughts regarding others. Every time you have a thought it directly affects you, it does not directly affect another. You are in you and you therefore belong to you. You can harm your own self by your *intent* to do harm to another. You can also heal your own self by your intent to do good for another. You are in a place where you are beginning to understand and focus on energy. Energy is what you are and energy is also what you will wish to change and move. You want the dense energy to move and allow space for the light energy. You want the dense energy to dissolve and allow time for "light" to take over.

When light has begun to take over there will be an unmistakable shift in awareness. This shift will be followed by a great increase in your vibrational field. As your electrical field begins to move faster and faster, you begin to access parts of reality that did not appear to you when you vibrated at a slower rate. Your vibration will literally begin to shake things up and move things around. Some things will be dislodged and moved forward in order to be released. The faster you vibrate the more you stir things up. When you stir things up, you may get a big headache or even the signs of illness. This is part of your vibrational field clearing itself and making itself free of debris. As this process proceeds, you will become accustomed to these shifts and you will know that ascension is taking place. Do not fear. You are simply falling apart in order to reassemble in a better way.

You will learn that as you begin to vibrate and clear certain debris, you may also begin to feel weak and out of energy. This too is due to the fact that your body is functioning at a higher vibration and, in doing so, is stirring up debris and jarring things around. As you learn to deal with these situations you may wish to remember to love you and to *allow* you to be who you are. This is part of who you are. You are not being punished, you are simply moving into clarity and to get clear you must remove all obstructions to clarity.

These obstructions are all right inside of you and you may clear them out of you and make things much better for yourself. This part of healing will take a bit of patience. Most of you are so low on patience that this may feel like a heavy burden that you will carry for a very long time. Actually, in the scheme of things, this is a very short period of time when you consider how many years and how many lifetimes you "took on" garbage and it is only now that you are beginning to peel away the layers.

As you move into this process I wish you to do so with gratitude and appreciation. Appreciate yourself for bringing you to this state of complete acceptance and complete awareness. You are not only moving ahead with determined innocence, you are moving ahead with trust and faith in a higher source of intelligence than you yourself now understand. You are not only one of the best, you are the only one. You are not only intelligence, you are information and wisdom. You are all things, and this part of you who is so tiny is trying to allow the rest of you to enter matter. Think of all that is written and all that has ever been written. It comes from the source. You may read a book and wonder about and debate over the brilliance and illumination of information given and it is all your information.

You each hold within you a treasure of intelligence. You each hold within you the key to unlock your brilliance. Your key is desire. You must desire God over all else. You must want God's will over your will. God is the key to your own intelligence. You will not see this series of books channeled by another as this is God's will at work. Liane allowed God to come in and use her body to do his will... not her will. She is willing to give up free will in order to live for God. This is how she created her connection. Have you surrendered completely? Do you do your will or do you do God's will? God's will may not look as good to you as what you believe to be your free will choices, but maybe the benefits are far greater than your limited mind can now accept. We will see how you do with your desire to allow God to take over. These are most interesting times, and all will know clearly at some point how things really work and what is really gold and what is fools gold.

≈⁂≈

As you begin to move along the path of least resistance, you will begin to see how you can best serve you by getting out of the way. It is only you who stands in the way of change. It is only you who stands in the way of ascension. It is only you who does not understand the workings on the highest levels of expanded awareness. In the light of this, I would suggest that you allow some other part of you to take the lead. It is best to allow God to lead you out of the darkness and ignorance that you are so deeply entrenched in. You are learning that even in your darkest moments God can assist you, and even in your most frail state it is God you lean on. Why not lean on God every day? Why not ask God for guidance every day? Not just when you are in trouble but before you get that far. Ask God to lead you every single day until you have completely surrendered to his wishes. This will be a good way for you to get to know God. If you deal with God on a daily basis you have a better chance of understanding your own God-self.

How can you possibly not wish to listen to God? How can you possibly not wish to do God's will? Has your own willfulness taken control? Is it that you no longer wish to hear what God wants because you are so caught up in what you want? Do not be a slave to control. Let go of your desire to control and you will have a better chance of letting God control and run your life. When God takes over there will be no control. When God takes over there will only be ease of movement and simple light. Nothing big, nothing dramatic. You are the one who is into drama. God is simply into God. God does not push around creation and God does not wish to control and lord over. Your concept of God is all wrapped up in good vs. bad and a Superman image. God does not wing his way into creation and become your great savior and hero. God knocks gently on your door and says, "Excuse me, but do you know that you are hurting yourself by not loving yourself?" This is more God's way, and it has little to do with your hero ideas and your judgment of what should or should not be changed.

For right now, as I look down on this entire situation, I would say that the greatest change necessary is not to stop war and not to stop killing. The greatest change necessary, as I see it, is a change in your distorted view of reality. Once you change how you are viewing it and labeling it "awful" you will give creation the opportunity to come full circle. Yes! When I started this series I said to you what you wanted to hear, which had a great deal to do with not harming others and that has to do with you. *You* feel, on a very big level, everything that you do. Do not continue to harm them because, in your present state, you are harming you. You are not in them you are in you and you perceive what you are doing as bad, and as long as you perceive something as bad it will be your reality.

I want a shift in perception. I want you to see only good in every situation. Thousands upon thousands of entities love to get a thrill. At this time those entities are coming into form to be mutilated or massacred in order to create excitement. Excitement seems to be the order of the day. Especially with the worldwide news coverage. An entity may enter and create a big dramatic death scene and have an effect or impact on millions. This is what is going on. A young boy calls wolf to see how many people will jump and run to his aid. You are acting out very big dramas with very big tragedies. You were trying to outdo one another and I am trying to keep you all calm so you will not create greater excitement. The bottom line is this. If people wish to kill and fight they will do so. You need not feel guilty about not taking part and you need not feel guilty about not being there to pick up the pieces.

This is a way of taking you out of someone else's drama. If they wish to continue reincarnating to get abused or to abuse it is none of your affair, ignore them. Yes! I did say ignore them. This is one of the most difficult subjects to teach because you have been taught to rush in and save everyone from themselves and from their situations. I lose more and more of you to this type of stress. Let them act out whatever they wish to act out, and you go upon your merry way with the wisdom and the knowledge that they are playful spirits who came in to call attention to themselves through their dramatic ability. Lighten-up! No one dies in a massacre or a bombing. It is impossible for any of you to die. Start thinking from spirit instead of from gut reaction.

Become spirit. Spirit says, "Love, breathe, live." Soul does not say, "Rush out and save everyone and everything." It is not natural to interfere in the creation of another. Tend your own backyard and allow the spirits to play at their war games or whatever other tricks they may use to get attention. Attention is simply energy running toward them. Keep your energy for you.

✻

You are very difficult to convince in certain areas. You find yourself believing in violence and so you call everything that has pain attached a violent act. Some acts that you call violence have nothing to do with violence. If an entity comes in to play at being a soldier, do you call what he does violence or war training? If an entity comes in to become a leader of a country and is put in a position to bomb a hostile nation, do you call what he does violence? You seem to pick and choose and make decisions based on who is morally correct. One may have your permission to kill in wartime as you believe it is for a very good and noble purpose. Yet if the same entity comes into your home and kills you, it is violent and awful. You have decided to tag it awful, so now it is being given the power of being offensive.

If you do not condone violence you will not call anything violent. It is all games, and when you get so upset you are giving energy and attention to those playful spirits who came in to get attention. Let them call "wolf" and you go on about your way. Do not buy into this game. You are all falling for it. You went to a movie and sat in the audience for so long that you began to believe the actors were playing real parts. They are just acting. It is not real. There is no obscenity. There is no injustice. There is no murder. There is no killing of anyone any time. Please begin to know this and you will all begin to calm down.

You are now at a very important turning point and this corner you are turning will lead you to peace. Do not get sidetracked and believe that you must go out and save the world. The only saving that can be done is done on a spiritual level by each individual soul. Each soul has been programmed to receive what he or she believes is best for his or her growth. Let them learn for themselves whether this is working or not. You interfere in business that is not yours. You do not belong in another entity's created reality.

I am trying to bring you back to your own God-self. You reside in you. You do not reside in another. You go home through you; you do not go home by saving others. You may wish to help, but at this time you do not know what is really occurring so how can you possibly know the best path to walk in order to assist? You may inadvertently create greater fear and trauma. You may create greater confusion and control or you may create greater tension and greater need for excitement.

You are all playing victims to some degree. Some just have it down better than others. This will all balance itself out as you each balance out internally. The best way to stop any violence is to stop naming everything good or bad and begin to believe in only good. Yes! It is good to see this war. It is helping these particular spirits work out their differences and work out their belief in being a victim. Look at the great job they are doing in this play. Isn't their performance magnificent? My goodness! They had me convinced it was real. Bravo! What good entertainment.

This is what you are watching. It is all a movie. It is entertainment. The more powerful souls give the greatest performance. Applaud the soul for his performance but remain in the audience. Don't get involved. Just pass through on your way to ascension. I want you to know that you too have your dramas that you are playing out and this is simply part of this process of letting go. Do not interfere when everyone begins to act out their stuff. It is literally coming up and out of them and they learn and grow in this fashion. So do you.

When you begin to clear and release your dysfunctional behavior you will wish for an audience also. It's no fun to be alone and act out a scene. You get no applause, no sympathy, there is no drama. You will learn that the more dramatic you are the more you will wish to get others involved in your thing. A good thing to do, in order to reduce the spread of being a victim, is to shut yourself in a room and act it out for yourself. My pen has done this on my advice and we found it quite beneficial. She could see what issues she was dealing with and still "act" out when necessary without involving others in her particular drama.

You will find that the more you involve others the messier things get. It's sort of like spreading peanut butter all over you and getting it on everyone you touch. When clean up time comes you have many to wash, whereas, if you act out alone you only have you to wash in the end. Do not spread your stuff around if it is not necessary. It only creates greater confusion and really stirs things up, and then everyone's "zing" starts to get all excited and begins to fly and I have no one who is calm and peaceful. So, if you want to help others you can do so by not spreading peanut butter on them. Know you and love you and allow you to act out as much as is necessary to free you from your emotional pain, which is caused by your belief in bad and awful. If you do not release your belief in bad and awful you will be held to it by your need for it.

❧

You are moving very quickly into a new way of viewing reality and all that you have previously believed will fall by the wayside. Think how much you have already changed your belief system and how far you have yet to go. This will give you an idea of how much you are going to grow and how little you will take into the future. Most of you will move into the future with little to no struggle once you have let go of your need to control your life. As you slip into allowing God to lead you, you will have time to rest and enjoy the ride. You will no longer feel the need to guard against all the things that you believe to be bad and dangerous, because you will no longer see anything as bad or dangerous. I know this is not the position you stand in now but you will.

When you get to this position where you can look around you and enjoy the moment, no matter how you once fought to control each moment, you will be in complete surrender. You will have given up the need for protection from yourself in favor of trusting yourself and what you create. You are moving into a form of trust that will allow you to be your very best. Trust is so close to love that you might say "it's the next best thing." When you begin to really trust you, you will be trusting life and you will be trusting God and you will be trusting love. You will know that no matter how your life is created it will be good. There will be no need to push at yourself to create better because you will know that you are creating the best for you.

When you get to this state of projected trust you will find that your creative skills increased one hundredfold. You will begin to know only goodness, and you will begin to know how you are projecting everything that you are out into the world. When this projection is seen as trust you will have created a world of trust.

You may begin to find that you grow to higher levels of awareness just having the ability to trust. This will allow you to know that you are creating your reality while you are in the "process" of creating it. As you begin to know that you are creating and how and when you are doing so, you will begin to slow down your need for punishment. You will no longer feel the need to push at you to be anything other than what you are, because you will know that it all comes from you and it is no longer seen as bad. As a matter of fact you will view absolutely everything as good.

This takes away any need for defense or for punishment. If you fear losing your job and you are in a tense environment you will simply lighten up, because you will "know" that if you are meant to lose this job it is good and will lead you to the next situation that is meant for you. This next situation will also hold good, and so you will learn to "go with the flow" of current that is moving through your life, and you will let go of this grip you have on everything.

You get very tense if you hold one position for too long. You are all very tense and now it is time to let go and trust that you are creating only good in your life. You cannot hold on for dear life and never let go of anything. What that says is: "I created good once, but I know I can't do it again so I'm not giving this up." That is not how you wish to live. It is also not moving into a future of created bliss. It is staying stuck to the old and being afraid that you have lost your ability to create good for yourself, and in order to believe in you once again you must learn to trust you all over again.

You once trusted you implicitly. Now you only trust what someone can guarantee for you. You want a promise of fulfillment on everything before you will trust. You are "afraid."

As you begin to process the information that is leading you into you, you will find that you are changing in very subtle ways. Most of your changing is taking place on a cellular level and you will not be consciously aware of it for some time.

As you move into the part of you that is most certain to become light, you begin to see from the position of this new part. You will find that you are not only becoming new, you are also becoming very different from what you once were. Some of you will feel this change in a very big way, while others simply note small changes here and there. For those who change most drastically it can be quite uncomfortable in the beginning. You may find it difficult to be who you are, as this change is so great that you are left with little to no connection to your former personality. If this is the situation you will be less and less likely to show off by proving how different you have become.

Some of you will find it necessary to say, "Look at me. I have changed and so can you." The intent will be to get attention and this intent in itself is enough to create some problems for you. The best way to handle change is to admit that, not only do you not understand what is going on; you also do not understand how you got to be this new you. This will allow you the space you need to grow without everyone focusing in on what you are doing.

Do not seek out attention. I know this is difficult for you because you are all so desperate for love and attention at this time. Some of you will learn to stay focused on growth and forget about glory. This need for positive appreciation and support is what leads you to want to say how well you have done. You are looking for approval outside of yourself and it is not necessary. Once you begin to change, you will not be so certain about your new position and can easily be pushed back out of this new position. Sometimes you may get pushed back further than you were before you took the step forward. Learn to accept you and you will no longer have the need to run to others for acceptance.

When you begin to truly accept you, you will no longer find it necessary to go out and save the rest of the world. In accepting you, you are actually accepting and embracing "all that is." It will no longer be necessary to save the rest of the world as you will have all of you and you are "all that is." When you learn to accept you and allow you to be who you are, you may still find it difficult to be accepted by everyone else. This is due to the shift in perception and not everyone will agree with how you are viewing creation. As a matter of fact, some may out and out disagree with how you are viewing reality. This too is your created perception of what is going on. When you first tell a child that babies actually come out of their mother's stomach the child may disagree whole heartedly. If that child has never seen a pregnant mother it will be very difficult to convince the child of such nonsense. He will need to figure this out for himself or somehow grow into this information.

So, my point is this. Does it really matter to you if the child believes you or do you jokingly laugh and allow him to discover his own reality in his own way? Why must it be necessary for him to agree with you or to know what you know? It is just you wanting attention. It is you wanting to be the wise one, the teacher, the one who leads. Let go of this need to be in control and you will no longer find it difficult to converse intelligently with anyone – regardless of his or her belief system.

When you have evolved to this level of thinking you will no longer yearn for someone to talk to, or someone you can relate to, or someone you can be yourself with. You will find that everyone has good to relate in his or her own way and on his or her own level. Learn to listen and stop trying to convince everyone that your way is better. After all, once you are God all ways are your way.

When you begin to move along your path to ascension you will be in a most remarkable position. With ascension comes all the hope and promise of everything that you know and have forgotten. With ascension comes love. With ascension comes the promise of return. What you are returning to is God/love/yourself. You have gone out in search and now you are returning to be whole. You are returning to be available to you. You are returning to be part of your own destiny.

Do you notice how bored you get when I write about you? You find you quite boring and unexciting. I write about angels or aliens and you want to know all about them. I write about you and you get easily bored and want to hear bigger news. You do not care about you so why would you want to read about what you will go through during transformation, or how you will feel? You simply want me to tell you everything that will occur outside of you. Then, only when you begin to "feel" these changes and they frighten you, then you may be interested to read about what will happen inside of you and how it may or may not affect you. For now I'll write it down and you may ignore it or use it. It is your choice.

So, as I was saying, you begin to feel hope with ascension, and this hope leads to a new belief in the future and how things may actually be changing for you. As you begin to discover more and more parts of you, you will begin to know you are indeed multidimensional. In other words, you are already there. You have already ascended and you live on many levels at once. The idea is to get you to realize that you have already been 'forever' and you will continue to be 'forever.' The trick is to get you to know it and to get you to allow you to be a multi-dimensional being without interference.

Why would you interfere? Well there are many reasons. For one thing you do not wish to be who you are. You do not wish to believe that you actually *know* everything and *are* everything. You prefer to believe that you are a pawn and a victim. It is time to rise up out of this role you play and to know that your dramatic role is simply a part that you are playing. When you begin to use this talent and ability for role-playing, you will shift from victim to God. For now you don't acknowledge how you create your roles, so how can you shift this power and use it differently?

You will find that as you begin the ascension process you are simply opening up to what is already there in front of you. These are not such exciting times of discovery as most believe. What you think you are learning and discovering has always been there. You are "there" but your focus is stuck in "here" so you think you are "here." It is like watching a slide show. You put in a picture and project it onto a screen and you are there. Then you put in a new picture and project it onto a screen and wow! – You are there. Now you must learn that you are the projector and you have the ability to create or manufacture all of the pictures and project them out. You can say you are here or you are there but you have always been. You are everywhere all the time and you have always been ascended, you just are not projecting that picture. Your slide projector got stuck and will no longer show you all that you really are, so now it is being repaired.

There are many possibilities, many dreams, many beliefs, many opinions. Save them all for when you learn how you are operating. I do not tell you what is right or what is wrong. There is no such thing and whatever choices you make will be good. I work with you from where "you believe you are." In this way I can assist you by changing your attitude toward what you "believe" you are seeing. As I said before, if an animal is in pain and caught up in barbed wire, the best way to help would be to calm the animal until you can begin to pull the barbs out and unwind the wire. If he pushes himself up to run or walk he may harm himself further.

What I say to you now is, "Yes, I know how great you are and I know how you can create vast fortunes of wealth and build huge empires, but wait. Wait until you know who you are so you will create from love and let go of further fear." A great huge empire built on mistrust and lack of love will carry its own problems. Stop pushing yourself up to walk until we can effectively remove all of your old problems. How will you know when you are ready? Easy! There will be no effort. There will be no pushing you at all. All of your life will simply flow as it has always done without your conscious awareness. You will not struggle. Life will give to you; you will not take from life what you want. This is true receiving and true sharing. Neither receiving or sharing are what you believe them to be.

※

I wish you to know that you need never be part of God. If you do not wish to open to the fact that you are God it is your own choice. You may wander this planet and never accept and it still does not change what you are. It simply inhibits you from knowing who you are. If you were born into royalty and were never told, you may not care. You also may not want to know. Maybe you are having too much fun where you are or being who you think you are. Maybe you are just too busy to be bothered, or maybe you don't want to be royalty because you don't know how to act if you are. Whether you choose to wake up or whether you choose to stay unconscious to your identity is totally up to you. The catch is – you don't know who you are so how can you know what you decided? How do you know what is driving your car? How do you know what direction your car is headed in, and how do you know what the purpose of your chosen direction is?

Two things are most important *if* you do not want to wake up now. One is that you ask God to drive your car and two is that, once you have asked, you allow him to do so. In other words, if you sit in the passenger seat do not give directions. You are ready to give up control but the *habit* is strong in you. Give the wheel over to God and sit back and relax. Allow God to make your life easier. Do not believe that God will simply leave you to struggle in your messes. Sit back, relax and know that God is sitting right there with you.

You are God and, whether you wish to acknowledge it or not, you are protecting, guiding and taking good care of you. Trust you. Trust God. Allow God to take over. Believe it or not, you will actually begin to feel the difference between God and ego. God's ways are soft and gentle and yet strong. Ego ways are demanding and pushing yet weak. You will begin to know the difference between strength and weakness. Weakness is not always as it appears and strength is also deceiving at times.

As you begin to learn more and more about your true identity, you will begin to see how you are powerful in your grace. Grace is the position of accepted trust that allows you to feel totally at ease "in" you. You will be in a state of grace when you no longer must "think," you simply "do" and you "do" with trust. This will be your ultimate goal on this particular path. Your goal is to reach a state of grace which is trust in God and trust in "all that is." As you turn this corner you will begin to collide head on with love. Love and grace go hand in hand as does trust and faith.

You will find that the greater your sense of right and wrong, the greater your pull away from grace. This is the "fall from grace." Sinning was not the fall. Mistrust and a belief in sinning became the fall. This is how you create: You do, then you judge, then you sentence to punishment, then you feel relieved of your guilt after you have served time for being bad, then you emerge a new, purged individual and you can once again live with yourself because you got your just desserts.

Well, things are beginning to change aren't they? Punishment is not strong enough anymore so you want stronger penalties for criminals. The crime system is breaking down because it is a direct reflection of your belief in right and wrong, and it must go. That is how creation works. You create it, and then it is acted out in front of your eyes for as long as it takes for you to get what you are really doing to yourselves. As you begin to fall apart and let parts of your belief system go, you will see systems fall apart because they were built by your belief system. Stop your belief in it and it stops. It's all very simple stuff really.

When you turn from dark to light you begin to sense that you are no longer your old self. You begin to believe that you are growing and ascending, and you also have your old parts or habits that will judge all that you are doing. Trust this process that is turning you from dark to light. Trust this knowingness that is just now beginning to surface. Know that you are safe, and know that all that is occurring is in accordance with this process.

Do not be afraid to continue. You will be moving even when you believe that you are not. You are being drawn back in to where you came from. The expansion process is complete and you are moving in. You have been expanding into space for so long that now you must reverse and go back into yourself. You have taken part in an adventure and now it is time to return. You are returning to your source. You are light and you are love. There really is nothing else. You made up all that other stuff by imagining it. You thought it by literally projecting it from you out into creation.

You no longer wish to create in this manner. You wish to return. I am not telling you to return so much as you are telling me (on many levels) and I am now letting you know what you have been letting me know. This is not God riding in on a white horse and serving you an idea of victory or a solution to your delusion. This is God telling you what you have been telling me.

You are so lost and fragmented and unaware of other you's that you can't possibly communicate with all of you. You are split and separate and I will help you become one. First you must look at how many of you, you think you are, and then we will be able to show you the illusion of separation. You are learning to return to you and to become one and this frightens you. You lose your sense of who is good and who is better and who is best. If you are all one you have no more separation and nothing to protect you from your thoughts. If you believe in separation you can name one person as bad and another as good, and you can make a friend of the good one and leave the others behind. If you are aware that you are not separate then you must acknowledge all parts of the whole. No one gets left out.

When you believe you are separate you may think whatever you want and not take responsibility for your thoughts. You may wish for someone to drop dead and not realize that your thought is in you and therefore it *affects* you and is constantly projecting "drop dead, drop dead." Now; if you realize how you are all one you will realize how every thought you think runs through you and, therefore, *directly* affects you. You are not outside your thought area. As a matter of fact you are the mechanism that carries your thoughts and is, therefore, most affected by them. So if you have a wish or a need or a thought for someone to go away, it is you pushing parts of you away.

Look at your mirror. If you do not like what you see you do not like you. If you push you away you are fragmenting you. Learn to embrace all parts of you. Learn to allow you to be whole by allowing all parts to exist and be free to express who they are. This does not mean accepting only those you understand. You cannot understand much at this time because you are confused. You will learn to understand after you have learned to accept.

This is your choice. You have chosen to return and I am simply letting you know since you have little to no communication with most of you. So, as you begin this return, I wish you to know that you will find parts of you returning and reconnecting. These are parts you left behind and they are now in need of your love. To heal you, you must heal all of you.

So, you may feel like you are going backward when you do this retracing to retrieve parts. Do not give up and believe that you are no longer moving in the right direction. Your direction is to God. Your path is well known and you always know what you don't think you know. Stay calm and be in a state of grace. Know that you will retrieve much of you simply by allowing you to be and not tagging parts as good or bad. You will learn, at some point, that much of what you dread and fear is actually much more conducive to your spirit than what you now so lovingly embraced. Let go of your need to hold on to the good, you may have mislabeled a few things and this too will become clear in time.

⧄

You are the one and only part of you that is led around by your ego. You are the part of you who does not know that your life is not at all your life. You are the part of you who was meant to wake up and allow the rest of you to emerge. If you do not wake up this time you will get to do this again and again until you are awake. It is like opening a jar that contains light. The lid is on tightly to preserve the light. We must continue to turn the lid until it breaks its seal. This will allow the light out. It will allow the contents of this jar to be known. It will also allow all contents to be looked upon.

As you open your jar you may find that your lid is stuck. You cannot get you "open." Keep trying. Every lid comes off in time. All light is set free in time. Maybe you got a really good seal on your jar to protect your light and now the seal is so good that even you cannot get into your own contents. Do not give up. You will release your seal of protection when you are ready. Everything will occur when you are ready.

Now, for those of you who have begun to break that seal, I wish you to know that your contents have great value and great insight for you. You will find that when you look upon your own light you will be looking upon you in a state of nakedness. Your ego will be stripped away, and your "will" will be put aside, and your darkness will begin to dissolve. Out of this transforming site will come your truth. You will see who you are. You will see how you were programmed to believe exactly what others wanted you to believe and, in seeing how you were programmed, you will be able to let go of your programming. I am constantly telling you to "let it go" because you are not part of it, you only "think" that you are.

You are the light that shines and you are not what is in the light, you "are" the light. To say that you are anything else is to fragment yourself and to cause yourself greater separation. You are not your fingers or your toes. You are the whole. You are not the part, you are the whole. You are not the one who observes, you are the observation. You are the totality of any given situation. You are not a fragment of anything. You are the totality of everything.

So, when you begin to "open" and to let you out of your confinement, you will find that you take up all space and time. You are everything and everything is you. You are connected to "all that is," and "all that is" spreads like liquid. "All that is" flows and blends and becomes one vast ocean of light, a sea of bright light is bringing you this series of books. A sea of bright light is coming up through this girl to share this information. It has not been easy for her. She has *felt* every word that has been written and her body has responded and transformed enough to continue to allow more to come through.

She is moving and shifting and changing constantly and she feels bad a lot! She is in her darkness in order to release it and she has been plunged into her darkness by the need to return to the light. Do not judge those who are confused and in a state of fear. They are moving to the light and the light is buried under all that garbage from your belief in bad. Stop believing in bad and wrong and stop judging others as being wrong. It is just your reflection of how wrong you believe you are.

When you begin to let go of your need to be right or wrong you will no longer require this information. You will no longer need a step-by-step directory of how to let go because you will not be holding on to judgment. But, for now, we will work within the boundaries and limitations you have set for yourselves. If you were in an unlimited state I could simply snap my fingers and say "transform" and, voilà, you would. It is not so easy when you are in your limitation. It is like telling a fly that is stuck on flypaper to simply "let go of it and you will be free." It is only easy if you are in freedom already. It is difficult from where you are because where you are is "in pain and debris."

So, I have come, by invitation, to walk you through your garbage so that you might clean out enough to enjoy living. You are doing well and this undertaking has been well worth the effort. Liane has agreed to continue and as long as she *allows* me to work through her I will.

❦

You will find that, not only are you changing and developing new traits, you are also becoming those new traits. As you spin faster and faster you will let go of these new traits as well and go even further *up* and out of all that you once considered to be truth. You are moving and letting go of a great deal and you will experience this in certain ways. Each individual will experience what is leaving and each individual will know his or her own truth. If you have the urge to look at another and say, "Oh, I see what you are doing," I wish you to stop. If that particular individual knows what he is doing he will not require you to tell him. If this individual does not know what he is doing you cannot possibly know. You can only know what you are doing because only you hold your view of reality.

If you tell another what he or she is doing you are putting your reality mask on that individual. Do not make someone into one of your characters. This is a way of sucking them into your reality and your drama. Let them stay in their own reality. They do not become what you think they are just because that is how you see them. What you see is not them. What you see is you. You are looking at you whenever you view the world. Try to remember that everyone is simply a reflection. You cannot tell everyone what you "think" they are. This does not work. You *are* what you think you are, therefore, you "think" you can project that reality out onto everyone else. You cannot. It will not work.

Now; here is what happens: you draw someone to you and then you begin to see this or that in them. The reason you are seeing this or that in them is because they too carry what you carry. You are all the same. So you begin to see this or that in them and it turns you off. You want to fix them or show them how much better things would be if they would only be this way or be that way. In essence, what you are seeing in them is a part of you that you are projecting out very strongly, and the more this part of you disturbs you the more of it you will project out. So now you get to see more and more how this individual disturbs you.

You are making other people the target of your disdain when, in actuality, it is just the stuff you are projecting out into or onto the world. The world is safe and in perfect harmony. The universe is safe and in perfect harmony. Stop seeing it from within your pain and confusion. It looks like pain and confusion to you because you are *in* you and that is what is being projected from you.

When you begin to project love and light, you will have the ability to only see love and light. You are simply learning to tune in to love. When you get you "in love" you will project love, therefore, you will see only love.

You will discover that you are no longer in fear and you will move forward from your stuck position. As you begin to move forward you may move into a new area with a new set of fears. Each time that you are allowed to face your fears and deal with them head on you will be allowed to clear them and move on to the next step. You are stepping very gingerly up the ladder of success. As you move up this ladder you will know more and more of you and this will allow you to let go of more and more of you. You cannot let go of it if you do not recognize what you carry. Do not get upset when you begin to come out of denial and see how much you actually do carry.

You will find that the greater your need to deny, the greater your need to release. Denial is a form of holding on. If you do not admit that you are playing a dysfunctional game you do not need to let go of the game. You may lie to yourself forever and not let go of your habits if you do not acknowledge the truth and come out into the light so that you might see how you are harming you.

Do you know that there is no danger except in your own mind? This means that all harm comes from within. All danger comes from within. No one ever harms you. Your fear of harm draws to you what you most fear. Your pictures in your mind create a vivid picture on the screen of your reality and you get to act out your fear of danger. If you believe in danger you will see danger. You will find that same fear in another and you will label them dangerous. This is you seeing your own garbage that has been projected out onto another. You see them as bad because they too possess "fear of danger" as you do.

When you possess fear of danger you constantly flash this to others who begin to avoid you because you become dangerous by believing in danger. What you believe in is what you flash to the world. If you believe in love you flash "love" to the world. When you learn how "you can only see in another, what you yourself are projecting onto them," you will see how your belief can get you loved, or hugged, beat up, or shot. It is all up to you and what you are "flashing" or advertising for.

After you have come to understand the dynamics of advertising, you will see how it "pays to advertise." Not only do you get what you advertise for, you also get to see how it all works. You will find that when you advertise strongly enough you will create a whole new world for yourself. The trick is to recognize what you have created so that you might enjoy it. You will find that as you begin to calm down and slow down you will be seeing your created reality. You will be seeing how you are creating peace. In many instances you will not know how to *accept* peace. It will feel "still" and you do not like the stillness. You are still hooked up to excitement and action, and you believe it is best to have a lot going on in your life. If you have nothing zinging around you feel worthless and bored.

You do not know how to accept peace because you have never known peace. You have elderly people who literally die because they do not feel useful. You do not have to be useful. This is a programmed belief. You do not need to work, or promote, or push to create, or strive for. It is not your job. Your job is to *be*. Stop pretending that life is wonderful simply because you are doing this or that. This and that have nothing to do with your inner peace. As a matter of fact, inner peace comes from doing nothing.

Stop pushing you to be successful and allow you to be peaceful. Stop moving. Stop pushing at you. Stop being afraid to stop. You are on this spinning wheel of creativity and you are so wrapped up in it that you are afraid to stop. You are afraid of *peace*. "Oh my God, what will I do if I have nothing to do?" This is a very big fear for you all and I wish you to become aware of what you are flashing because you are advertising for the opposite of peace out of a "fear of peace."

You will learn that not only do you not know how to embrace peace; you do not know how to live from moment to moment without a plan. You do not know how to be free and you are totally "caught up" in not being free. Freedom comes with knowing who you are and accepting all parts of you. To be limited is to not accept that you have the ability and capability to survive without work, without food, without money, without stress, without hatred, without fear.

As you learn to accept that your possibilities for survival do not depend on your job, you will learn that you may do whatever you wish and still live and enjoy life. You will learn that you may be guided into situations that are a letting go process and you will still survive. You will be taken care of by God when you allow God into your life. You will not live as you expect because your expectations are all fear-based and do not work in a love situation. When you begin to move into "unlimited self" you will no longer believe that you must struggle to survive. Struggle is war and does nothing to give you peace.

Peace comes with knowing that you are an unlimited being and, therefore, you can create from unlimited resources. When you send out the message that you can only survive by means of education and a good job you limit your created receptive ability to an education and good job. There are actually many, many other ways, but you choose to limit yourself because you cannot see – because you are not "free" to see – because you choose limitation. Be free! Begin to know that God will create for you. You are God and you do know how to survive and it is not cast in stone that it be done this way or that way. Go beyond limitation. Free up your God-self to begin to create for you. And when it comes do not judge it for if you do you will negate its power. Allow, accept, receive and know that all is well.

༄༅

*W*hen you begin to fall apart you will see everyone else falling apart. This is due to your ability to project you out onto everyone else. As you fall apart you will project this forward and what you will see (or read) when you look at the world is that everyone and everything is now falling apart. Reflections are very helpful in allowing us to see who we are and how we are doing. Now; when you begin to observe those who do not have it together it is best to understand that this is you, it is not them. Sometimes it will be most difficult for you to face your own truth but this too is acceptable.

As you begin to know more and more about who you are you will begin to observe this wonderful effect taking place. This will be the change of you. You will be riding high one day and very low the next. This is you getting unstuck. This is you becoming aware that you are moving up and down. When you begin to go through these highs and lows I wish you to remember that you are simply moving out of a stuck, controlled position.

In order to give up control you must feel as though you have no control. The degree to which you can give up is the degree to which you will lose control. When you begin to lose control do not be alarmed. It is you falling apart and this is good. It is no longer necessary to pretend that you know it all and that you have total control of your life. This is coming out of the lie. The lie is, "I am in total control and everything is wonderful." The truth is, "I do not know what's going on and I am falling apart." The greater the need to reclaim your control, the greater the need to continue the lie. When you begin to give up control you will no longer need to lie. You will be unafraid to tell the truth.

When you begin to tell the truth you will be working within the light. You will be within what I call God's love. You will be within what might be considered a state of grace. Give up the need to control and allow yourself to fall apart. It is not so bad as you believe. It will only show you how there is nothing to fear but fear itself. As you begin to realize how you are controlling you at all times you will begin to see how you push at you to do this or achieve that. Relax! Learn to allow the universe to give to you. When you feel like doing something – do it. When you don't – don't do it.

It is so simple and yet you make it so difficult. You make boundaries and set limitations for yourself and you use you up. You are wasting away in a world you do not understand when you could be truly happy and not doing a single thing you do not want to do. Someone taught you that "you have to," or "you should," or "shame on you if you don't," or "how dare you not do the good and right thing." There are a million of these axioms that keep you locked up inside a very limited reality. You are going to "free" yourself and this will be most uncomfortable at times. Do not worry. I said you are going to free yourselves, I did not say you are going to hurt yourselves. That part is already done.

Now; when you begin to free you up you will begin to feel like maybe you are doing the "wrong" thing. This is due to the fact that you have been strongly programmed to be a limited being, and to unlimit yourself and give yourself free rein to think for yourself is considered dangerous. You have rules for society because you cannot and do not trust yourselves. I am going to teach you to trust yourselves which is very frightening to you. Once you know how to trust yourself you will know how to trust God. This is a very big step for all of humanity. Humanity has never trusted God. That is why you always kneel in fear before an omnipotent Lord. I want you to learn to walk with God and talk with God and get up off your knees and out of your fear of God.

༺☙༻

You will begin to understand evolution when you begin to understand that it has little to do with what you see in your outer world and a great deal to do with you. Evolution is not how you develop better technology. It is about evolving into a new form or being. Evolution is about becoming whole through the process of becoming all. The process is the part that you feel. It is like you are growing and stretching. When you begin to feel aches and pains in the emotional body, as well as the physical body, you will be stretching and growing beyond your current belief. When you do this you broaden your perspective and with a broadened perspective you are allowed to see more. You are moving and rising and stretching in your perception to allow more light in. As more light comes in, it automatically starts bringing you into a new reality. The reality of light is not based on the same beliefs and feelings as the reality of darkness. The reality of light is very much free.

When you begin to free yourself from the reality of darkness you will begin to see how darkness does not let you see the whole picture. Darkness gives you a very narrow perspective. This is due to the fact that darkness is not all knowing and, therefore, focuses on what it sees, and calls that everything. When you come into the reality of light you will see how it does not focus on one point of view and it allows for all points of view to be expressed. Not only does it allow for all points to be expressed it encourages all to take part. This is the reality of light. Light does not shut out one point of view in order to hold one point of view that may be preferred.

Being in the light does not mean believing in one system at the expense of all other systems. You may find that you prefer the dark reality because it gives you the limitation of a single perspective. In other words, if you have or hold one belief you do not have room in you to hold an opposing belief. What you will learn is that you are all perspectives and all points of view and to allow them all acceptance is to be the "totality of." You are always the totality of any given situation and you are "all that is".

Therefore you are the "totality of." You are not limited to being one or the other. You are simply "all that is."

Light is the true reality and light contains all that is. All points of view are part of light reality and, therefore, accepted. You do not shut out or shut down any viewpoint as invalid because, in the light, all is valid and no one thing has preference over another. Everything simply is. There is no wrong way and there is no better way. There is only light. Light is the way. You are moving from darkness to light and this *shift* is very uncomfortable for you. It is as though you are a man who was locked in a very dark cell with no light coming in for hundreds of years. Now you are being set free and the cell door is unlocking but you have forgotten what freedom is and you are afraid to even push open the door. You do not know what is out there beyond that door and it frightens you. You feel safe and secure in your dark cell. You have always been here and you know how to live in the dark. You do not know how to live in the light and it frightens you.

When you begin to push at that cell door you may run back inside the darkness for safety until you finally learn to trust the light. You see, you do not trust the light. It is new to you and exposes you. You feel safer with walls of protection even if they are a cell you were once locked in. You will find that you fear exposure to the light. Light is truth and you have hidden the truth for so long that it is second nature to you. Now you will learn to hide no more. You will come out and see what is here waiting for you.

You will be well received by the light and it will only be up to you as to how far you will venture away from your dark cell. Be kind to yourself and allow yourself time to adjust. Do not push yourself forward and do not push yourself backward into the old way. Allow yourself to explore the light and to "feel" it. Do not force yourself to make any decisions regarding how you "feel." In the light your feelings will constantly move and change. Freedom allows them this movement. When you are free you become very "floaty" and flexible. Some will feel this as wishy-washy, especially those who are accustomed to strong rules to keep them from being wishy-washy.

So, as you step out into the light, allow yourself to get used to the idea of not being controlled and confined by your old belief system. Allow yourself to relax into this and by all means stay calm. Do not rush about telling everyone how you are a light being until you know what you are talking about. I do not say this to put you down but to save you greater confusion. When you begin shouting who you are to the world, you begin creating another reality altogether. For now, let's just keep it simple and say, "I know nothing. I thought I did but now I don't think I do." Something like this will help keep you calm and in balance until you can see enough to know something.

You are perhaps the most wonderful experiment yet. You are the one who was created to hold light so that you might carry light into the world. You carried your light in and now you are learning to leave it. You are learning to let go in order to leave the light in the darkness. You are learning to let go in order to leave the light in a dark world. As you leave the light in the world, the world becomes a lighter place. When the world becomes a lighter place it will no longer draw darkness to it. It too will shift into higher gear and begin to rise above the dense gravitation of darkness.

When you begin to allow all of your senses to take over you will begin to release your light. Right now you are holding control over your senses because you do not know how to use them properly. Anything that is sensory has a purpose that will assist in your rise. Your sensory perceptions are well thought out and well used. You simply ignore them. There are many parts of you that you ignore. Not only do you ignore sensory output you ignore sensory input. You believe that you do what you do because that is the way that you are. When you begin to listen to sensory input and output you will begin to know that there is a reason for most of what you do. You do not act out of non-reason. You do act out of reason. This, of course, does not make the reason a truth; it simply makes the reason a reason.

So; when you begin to see how there is a reason for ignoring your sensory perception, you will wish to evaluate your reasons and begin to include this part of you into your daily life. Everyone has ESP (extra sensory perception). It is just that most refuse to use it. It is, of course, out of fear. With ESP you may know in advance what is going to occur and with ESP you can also know what you are doing on another level of reality. With ESP you can even predict future events. ESP is normally thought of as dangerous.

No one really wants to know anymore how tomorrow will directly affect them or how they will die or how they will change. Most people want to hear that they get to keep what they already have and may be getting a little more. This is, of course, how most of you feel. Give me only what I want and nothing else. It is like a child who screams constantly for candy. If I were to give a child all the candy they wished for, as long as they wished for it, I would have a very sick child with bad teeth.

So; what do you do with a child who is so pre-occupied with getting his treats? If you are God you let him have just a little at a time while you change the way he views what he is asking for. Then he may grow out of his need for candy. God does not ignore your requests. God simply wants you to get what is best, and what is best from God's position (which is quite high I might add) is not necessarily what looks good from your position.

You are beginning to move into a phase whereby you may want to reconnect with your sensory input and output. This will allow you to know why you are behaving the way you are. With this knowledge you will be free to reopen parts of yourself – the more intuitive parts who will lead you gracefully out of your habits and addictions. There is no sense in repeating a situation over and over again, when you can simply plug into your own sensory input and see what messages you are picking up and what is triggering you to react to another's response to you. You are creating a pattern of reaction to reaction, and someone needs to stop reacting and begin to *feel* what is going on.

You think you know what is going on in the lives of others but you do not. You only think that you do. So you react or respond to what you think is going on, and you are actually responding to your own perception and your own reactions. So now you respond inappropriately and the other person is confused and also responds or reacts inappropriately. This, of course, is due to the fact that he or she does not respond to who you really are, because he or she does not really know who you really are as he or she is not *in* you. So now he/she is responding to how you are responding and this confuses or upsets you, so you respond back again and.... Well... you can see how confused you all must be.

So; I will clean you out and open you up to your own ability to see who you are. This is by far the greatest gift I can give you. I know you are screaming for your candy and other goodies, but this is the "gold."

❧

You are about to embark on a remarkable journey into your own inner self. This journey is brought to you in order to allow you to know who you are. I know you get tired of me harping at you to learn about you. You don't like being you, so it is not surprising that you don't wish to look at you. However, at this time I am asking you to overlook your dislike of self and begin to explore yourself. See what you think in every situation. See how you look at every situation and see how you respond to every situation. Do you love and accept all that occurs? Do you find the gift in all that occurs? Do you find the gift in you? Do you understand that you took on darkness to serve you? Do you understand that darkness has its own place? Do you understand that darkness is not bad or wrong? Can you *allow* everything to be?

When you learn more about yourself you will begin to see how you can use all that is God. Darkness is not the absence of God. Darkness is simply taking what is light and twisting it into darkness. Darkness is taking what is already God and calling it dark or awful. If someone dies in your world and is reborn in another, you scream about how awful it is that so and so was shot. It is not awful. It is not dark. You call it dark but does that make it so? You say it is not God's way but does that make it so? "God does not kill" you shout, but does he kill? Does God not take up all time and space and, if he/she does, does this not mean that God is not only he or she, God is *all* that exists. And if God is all that exists, is he not killing and robbing and violence and all those things that you judge and tag as awful? And if you judge and tag them as awful, this too is God. You are creating God. You are the one who is God and you are afraid to admit that you are. You are afraid to look at you and you are afraid to be you.

You are the one who entered this dimension of illusion to spin dreams and make up stories. It's fun and games. All of it is fun and games. You are not here because you are God. You are here because you are trying to forget who you are. You wanted to get away for awhile. You wanted to retreat from your position in life. Your position as God was just a little too big. You wanted something smaller and a little less – if you know what I mean.

You wanted to be able to become whatever you thought: "Let's create a movie with good guys and bad guys. Let's create a movie where everyone is totally immersed in their role. Let's get this movie on a big screen and show everyone how great we are." This is how you created. You did not intend to immerse yourselves and never again reveal to yourselves your true identity. You are coming out of your drugged state now and you do not belong re-immersed. You are waking up and you are confused and you do not know how to get out of your role.

You have been role playing for so long now that it has become a major part of you. You talk the part and walk the part and act the part, and this is what I want you to look at. Who are you pretending to be? If you can see your mask or your role it will help you to let go of your role and become who you are. Once you can identify who you are playing, it will assist you in knowing that it is simply a role and it is no longer necessary to play your role.

When you begin to un-play your role, or, in some cases, replay your role you will begin to see how you no longer require role playing. You will see how you are ready to come out of your movie and observe it from a new perspective. Then, once you are ready to give up the role of observer you will rise above that position to a position of non-interest in the role or the movie. At that point you will simply leave the role playing and the observing to those who are still intrigued, and you will move on to a new perspective.

This perspective will be one of not getting involved in either game. You will function with love to guide you, and you will only do what you "feel" like doing and you will literally be moved by feelings. It will be effortless movement with no push, or strain, or worry about what is right or wrong because there will no longer be right or wrong. There will be no need for you to create darkness by calling everything that you do not approve of dark. Darkness will have left your life because you will no longer be *using* it. It will no longer be of service to you so you will move on to other endeavors.

When you get to this point in your evolution or your spin up and out of darkness, you will see how you created it all by your "belief in." You will see how, when you were role playing, you made or called certain things dark so that you might have more drama in your little movie. You now need drama to convince you that you are alive. This too will change. When you learn the true value of living, you will know that drama is just a way to keep the "zing" flying all over so you can feel like you are doing something.

Don't worry, you will get the hang of how all of this works and you too will want to be up and out of your movie and even up and out of your audience. You will move above such games and, in doing so, you will no longer find it necessary to condemn anyone or anything to the darkness. Nothing is really wrong or bad or awful; not you, not your neighbor, not the world, not the game and certainly not the God who created it all. Look at all of life from a higher perspective and you evolve up out of the darkness. The darkness is simply your own belief in it. Nothing else exists. You are making it dark by calling it dark. Stop calling it dark.

⊰⦚⊱

You are moving into what I will call the fourth dimension and you are learning to focus on everything from a new perspective. Once you settle into this new perspective I will show you how to let go of it and move on to no perspective. If you have no perspective you have no position. If you have no position you are free floating. A position-less being is an unstuck being.

So, do not be upset if you can no longer sound intelligent because intelligence thus far is based on definite knowledge of how something is. This freezes everything into a locked position and if you cannot know everything, everything will be allowed to move. When you know intellectually that this is so, or that is proved to be so, you will stop it dead in its track. You will not allow it to be anything else for you, as thought or belief creates for you, not for your neighbor but for you. You block yourself from all possibilities by knowing all the answers. This is very limiting and gets you very stuck.

I want you to be dumb. What you call dumb is, "not knowing the answers to the questions." What I call dumb is, "knowing the answer and not allowing every answer to work." So, for now, play dumb. Let go of knowing and begin to not know. This will get you out of positionality, as you will be letting go of your position on any given thought or idea. This will allow all thoughts and ideas to flow. This will allow you to at least become a tiny bit intelligent.

When you begin to see how you have been programmed since the beginning of time to go in a certain direction and now for the first time you are being required to reverse direction to seek out God, you will be willing to be dumb. You will enjoy being dumb and holding no position and no set belief. Rise above the world of "this answer is right and all others are wrong." The truth is that all answers are correct if they are believed strongly enough, because what is believed is what moves matter and creates reality.

I will tell you now that if you take one position strongly it will change at some point and you will be, eventually, knocked out of that position. You have a very old saying, "the bigger they are the harder they fall." This is true of big beliefs or truths. The more certain you are that your belief is right, the bigger you get in your belief. I do not want you to *hold* any beliefs. I want you to allow all ideas and thoughts to be acceptable. Allow everything to be what it was meant to be. It is all just energy running up and down, and you change it and stop it and take on some and push away others. Take on nothing and push away nothing. Allow it all to be.

When you begin to understand how energy works, you will begin to see how you do not have the intelligence to work with it and not fight it at every turn. Once you grow accustomed to knowing who you are you will begin to see how you not only do not rise above positionality, you are so stuck in so many beliefs that it may take me forever to dig you out. You are being uprooted and it may leave you a bit bewildered and confused and best of all... without answers!

You will learn that you are moving into an area of total acceptance. This means that you do not judge nor do you besmirch the character of another simply because he or she does not live by your rules and your beliefs. You are very quickly learning that you control your limitations by accepting them as true for you. Now you are about to learn that you no longer have the need to limit yourself and so you will let go of your need to limit others. When you no longer find it necessary to limit others you will realize how you are letting go of limitation and becoming an unlimited being. This is how you rise up. This is how you ascend. You begin to rise above your current limited thinking and you begin to know how you are all things and all possibilities.

You will find that the greater your ability to "live and let live" the greater your ability to ascend. When you begin to allow others to be right and correct in their way of thinking, even though it is totally opposite of how you see things, you will begin to allow you to be right and correct in yours. The actual reason you fight for your rights is out of fear of not getting and fear of being wrong or told you are wrong. When you are told you are wrong you feel like you are not accepted. When you are not accepted you feel like you are not loved. When you are not loved you go crazy because you do not love you, and your need to talk everyone else into loving and accepting you comes from the need to love yourself.

So; if you can allow yourself to allow everyone to be right and correct in their way of seeing things, you will be on your way to allowing you to be right and correct, which means you won't have to argue because you will be allowing you to be right and them to be right. You will be seeing above positionality and you will be moving closer to oneness and away from separation.

This does not mean that you will be surrendering your free will to others. You may view this as you would food. One of you may like potatoes and another pasta. When one says, "I think potatoes are the best food ever," you don't reply with, "How can you possibly say that when everyone knows that pasta is best?" Give up the need to be right but do not give up you to another's will. Do not force you to eat potatoes just because they please another. Tell your friend how you agree that potatoes are great but you love pasta. There is no need to debate over such trivialities in life. Nothing really matters and everything is an illusion anyway. So; stop struggling and spending all that energy trying to live everyone else's life and use that energy to live for yourself.

You are not so very far away from you. You are your goal. Retrieving your innocence is what this is all about. When you have retrieved your innocence you will no longer care about right and wrong. When you were tiny you didn't care, it had to be taught to you. You were innocent and it didn't matter to you who did what as long as you had a thumb to suck on. You were very happy in your ignorance and then you began to receive what is called training, schooling, education, learning, intelligence.

This is the end of that type of programmed intelligence. This is the beginning of illumination and it will assist you in your rise as did the teachings of right and wrong assist in your fall. You wanted to go down so you shifted down. Now you want to rise or go up so you shift up. This is how you do what will get you to your next step. This information is not meant to be held on to it is meant to flow. What I teach today gets you to step number two, and to get you to step number three I may have to take all of this away and give you all new information. So, how can you yell how correct you are in what you are learning and how wrong everyone else is? You are simply being programmed to assist you in a step you wish to take. Maybe your neighbor already took this step and is working on the next step. You have no way of knowing where anyone else is because you do not know where you are.

❧

*F*or the first time you will know love. You will be allowed to feel love by feeling how to accept all parts of you which indicates that you are accepting all parts of God. You are learning to accept and to grow and to know how to be "all that is." To be "all that is" you must allow "all that is" to be valid. You cannot cut out or cut off certain parts of God and only accept your truth and condemn all other truths. This is not God. God is all and all is God.

So, when you begin to think how your belief is right and your thought system is right I wish you to remember that everyone else's thought system and belief system is right also. There is no wrong, there only is. Everything simply is and all ways create. Just as you create from marble, or cement, or flower, or paint, or wood, or clay, or seed, or silver, or gold, or stone you create from you. You are the source of your created efforts and your source is all the same. No one has a different source. No one is better than or worse than. You just get in moods and say, "that's awful," or, "I should have done it this way instead."

You are learning now that you do not need to criticize or correct. Learn to allow all to be. In this you will be allowing you to be. This is what occurred. You were creating and you did not understand what you created so you called it stupid, or dumb, or ugly, or a waste of time. Then you put it down or threw it away. Two hundred years later someone found it and smoothed out the edges and said, "Wow, I will keep this and call it a wheel." You were just too dumb to know what you were criticizing.

At this time, and from the position you hold in darkness, you are just too dumb to know what you are creating, so please do not judge you or your creation. Allow creation to be and allow you to be. It's also a good idea to allow everyone else to be because you are really in no position to judge anyone or anything as not good enough or not smart enough. Allow everyone and everything to be and see how it evolves. If you do not see more clearly in two hundred years I will grant you permission to accept without seeing. For now I want you to see how you judge and criticize and put others down on a daily basis. This, of course, means that you are judging and criticizing and putting yourself down on a daily basis.

You have decided that you know best, and you love when someone comes to you for advice. You get to feel like you have the right answers and you are superior. Well, this is not the case. As a matter of fact the more you tell others "how it is" the more stuck you will become in "how you think it is." It is not how you think it is. It is how it is. You are and it is. There is nothing in between and nothing bigger or better or less or worse. You are confused and in darkness, and in your struggle to save yourself you are dragging you down and trying to get others to follow. Why not wait until you get to know something before you begin telling everyone "how it is." This will allow you to go forward and not get "stuck" in a certain position.

You will find that as you learn to see how you are behaving, it will assist you a great deal in moving forward and letting go of old programs and unnecessary garbage. You don't need to be right to feel good and you don't need to constantly keep score of who is smarter. You are all in the same boat. No one knows who they are or how they got here or how they will leave. Give up this competitiveness. You are competing against your own self and saying one part is right or better-than and that the other part is wrong or less-desirable-than. The truth is that all parts are equal and all parts serve a purpose.

When you begin to understand how all of this works you will no longer feel the need to show off by showing off how much you think you know. You are acting like you know the answers because you are so insecure and unsafe, and in your insecurity you feel unsafe. So you puff yourself up and tell others what is best and what will save them when what you really need is to look at your own self and save your own self.

As you grow and develop into what you are you will learn to allow everything and everyone to be who they are. You will know that the alcoholic is on his way to learning in his own way, and that the drug addict is on his path to ascension, and that the guy who just shot twelve people is really getting to learn and grow. He may even pass you as he is taking some very big steps in his path to understanding creation. Stop sitting in judgment of everyone and everything. It is one of the least acceptable things that you do. Everything is simply a game. All tools are learning tools. You are all creating drama so that you might learn to evolve and grow into something other than what you are. You know that you are more, and you use creation to attain certain levels of awareness so that you might come out of the darkness.

Who is really in the darkness, is it the guy holding the gun or is it the one who judges him for holding the gun? Think about it. Who has more fear – the guy who pulled the trigger or the guy who is horrified watching the scene? Maybe he pulled the trigger to help you get over *your* fear. Maybe someone shot someone just so you could evolve out of your fear of death. Think about it. Are they killing one another because it's fun and no one dies or is it for you, to help you get over your fear of death? Maybe it is both. Maybe the ones who are shooting it out and killing one another are actually having a very good time, while assisting you in your evolution out of your fear of death.

Not everything is how you think it is and there are a great many souls who will assist you now in many, many ways. Watch how you judge and what you judge. This will assist you in seeing where you are in your evolution up and out of fear. If there is no fear of a situation there will be no judgment call. Let go of fear and know that God is all things and God will insist you in many, many ways.

*W*hen you first begin to know who you are you will feel a bit confused. You will begin to see how you do not own your own life and you do not control your own being. When you get to this point of discovery you will see how your will to do this or that has been taken over by something more powerful. And what could be more powerful than the will? There are many things. In some instances it is the choice that was made before you entered your body. Yes, some choices were made well in advance and you are in accordance with what is known as your divine will choice. Others are made as you go and are frequently changed as you develop more and more quickly into your new self.

As this development takes place you begin to feel how you seem to be losing control of many aspects of you. Something else is taking control from you. This is the divine intervention that you have asked for. Do not be upset if you are not allowed to fulfill your normal routine. We are breaking all habits at this time so that you might learn the difference between want and desire and addiction-to.

You will find that as you learn to follow your heart you will no longer find it necessary to follow a set routine, which is basically locking you into a rut. It gives you little flexibility and it allows you to sink into a routine that becomes inflexible. It is stifling you and you do not require routines. You need only do as your heart directs and you will be leading a good life for you. Do not lock yourself into a necessity. It is important to do what you like doing and not force yourself to do what you do not wish to do. It is you pushing and shoving you. Do you see pushy people in your life? It is you pushing at you to do this or do that. Give yourself a break. You have a tendency to get on treadmills that lead you nowhere. You force yourself to follow a routine day in and day out so that you may have control over you. I want you to let go of control and learn how to *enjoy* doing the things you do. You need not force you to do anything.

Yes, I know; if you do not have a routine you may not get it done. Stop doing everything by the clock. There is no time. You are not lazy; you were simply taught that to lie around is lazy. Laziness is okay. Be lazy and fantasize and dream. Be all parts of you. Do not shut down everything that is part of your beingness. Allow yourself to sleep as late as you like. Take naps. Dream, dream, dream. You create best when you are asleep. Stop judging getting up at noon. You all want more energy and more time in your day... and why? Because you do not know how to simply be. You have lost your ability to just "be."

I want you to begin to see how much you control and push and shove you around. If you were your body and your emotions and your feelings, wouldn't you break down from all this pushing and shoving? Do you feel victimized by the world? Do you feel unsafe and insecure? Who wouldn't? If you were constantly pushing and shoving someone they would either leave or fight back. This is how your body responds. It fights back until it is exhausted and then it breaks down and gets sick, so you pump down some more vitamins and pills and force it to go on. Stop this nonsense. This is not balance. You do not need to take anything to make you feel better. Stop pushing at your body to perform and allow it to simply be. It was once in perfect working order. It ate what was natural for it to eat and it eliminated perfectly on its own. Now it is so full of garbage and toxic waste, and you push it even more and breathe pollution and eat pollution and force it to get up and move, move, move.

Did you ever see someone force an animal to keep moving when it was breaking down? It is not a pretty sight. Some people beat people to keep them going, I think this was once called slavery. Now it is expected that you perform to your peak. Competition is very big and you don't want to fall behind and get left out so you continue to compete. Give it a rest. Give competition a rest. Let them leave you behind in the dust. So what! Big deal! Is it really important or is going back to the light more important? If you chose the light you will be changing, and you may have a difficult time letting go of your need to zing around and stir up your excitement and your pride. You may have a difficult time letting your ego go. You may have a difficult time just being when you are forced to just "be." I know it is tough for you but you will learn how all of your programming has led you in one direction, and now I must lead you back in another direction just to give you back your balance.

Do not worry. You do not need control of you. When perfection comes back you will see the most wonderful changes. All life will become play and you will not be pushing at and shoving at you to do it. You will be loving it. You will be as the children who hum and sing and play because it is fun. You do not require rules and structured play time. Do what comes naturally when it comes naturally. You are not a machine to be programmed and controlled, you are a light being. Give that being a chance to come forward. Allow the light to do what it does best. Let go of your control and begin to know how you are light, and to bend light is to change it into something else. You are bending and pushing the light away. Learn to allow the light to be you. Do not judge these changes when they come. You are falling apart and this is good.

❧

You will find that you are most concerned about nothing. Whatever you are fighting for or struggling for or arguing over is nothing. None of that matters. It is unimportant and it will fade away when you stop arguing with yourself and begin to allow yourself to simply be. It is not necessary to struggle with your own self. This battle within has been keeping you at odds for such a long time that you no longer know how to live without this struggle. It goes on inside of you and is caused by your belief in one way being right and another way being wrong. Do not allow this struggle to take over. It is already projecting out into the world and being reflected back to you.

When you learn to change, do not hold on to that technique by which you change, as it may be only one step in the ladder up. Once you discover a learning technique or tool you do not have to use it your entire life. This is not growth. Growth is when you can let go of things and move on to the next. When you are just entering the fifth grade you feel dumb and need lots of help. When you have finished the fifth grade you feel smart and on top of things. This is when I will push you out of the fifth grade and into the sixth, so that you can learn more and see how you really didn't know as much as you thought you did.

This is how I teach. When you get too cocky and think you know it all I will step in and say, "Okay smarty, look at what you know nothing about." This will assist you by keeping some perspective about yourself. Most of you have no perspective at all regarding yourself. You think that if you know more, or something different, you are smart and everyone else is lost or slow. This is not true. Some are here to evolve and some are here to assist. Since you don't know who is who I suggest you hold your confidence and cockiness to a level of acceptable tolerance. Do not start shouting how you have insight when what you have is nothing compared to what is available. You do not know where you stand in the scheme of things and you sometimes dig yourselves in deeper by your lack of awareness and insight.

So; for now I will ask you to shut up, be quiet and think peace. Do not run around with an attitude of superior education because, for all you know, everything you have been learning may be a lie. You are simply being reprogrammed, and to shove this at others is just as silly as shoving the original teachings of good vs. evil at others.

You are learning and as you learn you grow and you change. You are being guided to know who you are; you are not being guided to know who your neighbor is. Your neighbor is simply your mirror and will show you what you need to change in your life. What if you are the only one who is messed up and needs this information? Do you put a bandage on everyone you see just because you needed a bandage? I think not. Stop trying to fix everyone else. In fixing them you are creating another reality altogether. Stay with you. Know you. Seek only to heal you. You are God. Focus on letting God in you; do not focus on selling God to everyone else.

This is exactly what you do. You wish to put you on everyone else because you do not care very much for you. You teach to love and yet you can't love you enough to keep you. You constantly send you out to be with everyone else and fix everyone else. Keep you for you. Stop pushing you on everyone else. Your ways are part of you. Use your love to keep you. You must learn to love you and hold you in place in that love. Stop pushing you out on the rest of humanity. Stay in you. Love you in you. Do not stray outside of you. Hold on to your love. You have held on to fear for so long and now I want you to hold on to love. Grip it tightly and hold it to you. Hold love in you. Keep yourself close to you. Keep yourself in you and keep all parts of you in your love.

You will find that it is okay to be stingy and to withhold you for you. You are a gift to you and you are the one thing that no one can ever take from you. Learn to know you and embrace you, and then hold you very close to your heart and never let you go. You will learn that this is you lovingly accepting and embracing all parts of you. Do not push at you to move. Stay still and hold on to you for dear life. You are your Christ child. You are God. You are Buddha; you are all the great gods and goddesses. There is no one more lovable than you are. Hold you. Keep you. Know you. Stay in you.

You are learning at this time how you are not meant for others you are meant for you. You are meant to be your own greatest gift. No one else has one of you. There is no such thing as another you. Oh, there may be many you's in you, but you are your one true gift. You are all of you and all of you is yours. You own you and you need not share any part of you. You may keep you safe or you may put you outside of you to struggle with the illusion of the world. I suggest that you keep you very close to your heart and you build huge walls of protection around you so you are safe. These walls are walls of love. These are not walls of fear to keep everyone out. These are walls of love to keep you "in."

You are the most remarkable human in that you are totally unconnected with who you are. You have dreams that you cannot understand and you do things and do not know why you do them. You are literally run on impulses. You are wound up so tightly with these impulses that you do not know what is you and what is not you. And you will begin to discover that not only do you create all that is occurring, you also create you. You are reshaping you as you go. You are dropping off parts that you no longer need and you are tuning in to what you do need.

You are very much in a position to assist in your own ascension yet you do not know who you are or what you do. You are a paradox of known and unknown. You are a mixture of truth and lies. You are "all that is" and you are nothing at all. You are everything and yet there is nothing here. You are most wondrous and remarkable. You are the darkness and you are the light. The darkness is the unconscious and the light is the conscious. You are every part of God and every part of creation. There is one catch. You are not only 'not' here you do not exist. You are a dream and you are God's dream.

When God began to dream he/she/God did not wish to be so lax as you might think. God wanted a certain flow to this dream and so he began to allow parts of his dream to wander off in a new direction. These parts became a little more moving than other parts and they also would return once they were projected out. It was like discovery. The dream would unfold and then it would return to its original start position so that it did not continue to wander and roll around in time.

As God's dreams became bigger and allowed for greater movement they were allowed to wander for greater lengths of time and to cover more space before returning. Then, as things really began to move, God was able to send out dreams that stayed put for endless moments before they returned, and they often took on a life of their own and began to feel more real than reality. Then the dreams were sent out in greater force to allow them to discover more movement, and these dreams returned much later but did not seem to remember how they were sent out or why they were returning.

Next it became apparent that to send out large movements it was best to "push forward" and this would propel these movements out into time/space. As this "push forward" took place it was received as a disconnection. It was not received as it was meant. With this perceived reception of the push came resentment. This particular dream now carried a huge charge of resentment and when it went out it perceived itself through the resentment of the push. This was not a violent act but was perceived as such by the dream mass. As this dream returned it held its resentment against its believed villain for being "pushed out." This, of course, created our first bad guy. You got it! God is the original bad egg. God is the original perceived bad guy. God did something that was judged as bad and this created your belief in bad, and this resentment is what is dragging you all down and tearing you apart.

It is not so much that you resent being the dream it is more that you resent being pushed out of God. This was not a villainous act. It was a simple matter of inflow and outflow. "In comes the good air, out goes the bad," comes from this belief. It is not good or bad it is all just "the flow," breathing in and breathing out, flowing forward and returning back. It is not wrong, it is not bad. You perceived yourself as being "pushed out" of God and you have been "feeling" rejection ever since. Let go of resentment and rejection will disappear with it. You are no longer being "pushed out," you are now returning and this is good.

⚜

You are now beginning to "feel" the shift that will set paradise in motion. You are beginning to know how you are not everything you want to be, you are simply everything that you already are. Everything that you already are is what makes you be you. What you are becoming has little to do with what you already are. You are not only 'not' what you thought; you are not even aware what you thought. Once you see how you are totally "made up" and not at all real, you will begin to see how you do not require anything in the way of needs. You have already met your needs simply by being. A being does not require directions on how to exist. A being is existence and a being is what he/she is. They do not 'become' simply because you finally realize how you are this being. This being has always been you and this being is most aware of you. You, however, have not been aware of this being for some time. You are too lost in your illusion to see how you have always been supreme and you have always been spirit. It is as when you dream or take a very powerful drug. You forget who you are.

When you dream you begin to go into another dimension and you forget all about this you who is asleep on your bed. You are not "focused" on the you who sleeps, you are focused on the you who is traveling and seeing other adventures. You are not concerned at all with the body who sleeps as you are totally absorbed in the sights and sounds of your dream. This is how you create. You visualize and imagine and then you move into the scene. You create it and then you get involved in it. It is time to come out of this dream. It is time to become the one who is dreaming and let go of the illusion. It is time to remember that you are drugged and dreaming. It is time. Do not waste your time trying to figure out why you did it. Accept it as you would accept falling asleep. You fall asleep when you need to sleep. You fell into the dream as part of sleep. You do not consciously say, "I am going to dream such and such," that is, not unless you are controlling your dreams.

Sometimes it is best to stop controlling everything for a while. Let all be presented to you and you will feel how you are receiving rather than in control of and on top of every situation. You may learn a great deal by letting go of control. It is not easy for you as you are all programmed to rise, get dressed, eat, rush to work, come home, eat, go to bed. What would you do if spirit took over your body and you couldn't rush around? What would you do if you didn't feel like or couldn't seem to control you enough to get you dressed? How would it feel if you stayed in bed for days for no reason other than no desire to get up and go? You would call this sick and I would call it a welcome change.

When you begin to see how you are no longer being led around by your programming you may begin to find yourself led around by your spirit. Do not be surprised if spirit wishes to make a few changes. After all, there is nothing quite like a "freed spirit."

∻

You will learn that as you begin to be all parts of you, you will be recognizing your own identity, and you will be allowing your identity to be who you truly are and allowing any false identity to slip away. You are very much in charge and you are losing your grip on being so. You are beginning to see and feel how you are when you no longer belong to fear. Fear will tell you that, "you must do this or you have to do that." Spirit will say, "it does not matter and who cares." Fear will tell you to, "be strong and stand up for your right," and spirit will say, "it does not matter and who cares." Your fear will tell you to, "take charge and keep going at any cost," and spirit will tell you that, "it does not matter and who cares."

When you begin to listen to your spirit you will find yourself being drawn to neutral ground. You may also find yourself being forced into situations to show how you "don't care and it doesn't matter." When you begin to learn how to create without control you will be allowed to see how spirit can take charge, and it will be none of your business as to how spirit handles any given situation. Once you begin to accept spirit as the one who is leading you, you will be allowed to see how spirit may not think as you think and spirit may not wish you to do things as you have been doing them. When you begin to follow spirit it will be difficult. You are accustomed to being in charge and you hate it when you think you have lost control. You will all wish to know that you do not know what is going on, so how can you possibly figure everything out and make decisions based on your assessment?

Once you begin to know more about spiritual development and spiritual evolution, you may begin to comprehend the value of following spirit. Spirit is not what you think. Spirit is not a ghostly part of you who pops in to check on you from time to time. Spirit is the part of you that runs the energy to your heart and your valuable organs. Spirit is in essence your life force energy. Spirit is always in you or you would not be here now. You would be nowhere which is not easy to define here, so I will tell you that you do not have a soul, you are a soul. You do not have spirit you are spirit. It is who you are. It is your essence, your light, your truth. Spirit is all that you truly are when you let go of all the garbage that you believe you are.

As you begin to show off your spirit and let go of your ego you will feel humbled. Humbled is good. You hate being humbled but it is so good for you. It gives you a new perspective and allows you to see from a softer and kinder perspective. Usually you get humbled, and it upsets you so much that you get your anger back up again in order to get out of being humble. You feel best when you are on top of situations because you have always been taught to fight, fight, fight. No one ever taught you to surrender, surrender, surrender. Sounds awful to you doesn't it? How can you be strong and the ever convincing good guy hero if you are humbled and not on top?

You will learn that not only do you require a little humbling right now; you also require a big surrender. So; I would suggest that you allow yourself to eat humble pie. It is the food of kindness and thought. You usually plunge ahead and do what makes you feel good, and most of what makes you feel good is due to being on top and feeling better than, smarter than and more sure than. These are all traits that you admire and yet you are not doing yourself a service by buying into this "better than" theory. It is just as destructive as the "not as good as" theory. You are not smarter, you are not dumber. You are all one and you don't know what and who you are, and when you look at everyone else you call them as you see them and you are simply looking through your own distorted truth. Give it all up. Stop pretending to know anything and admit you are helpless and asking for God to get you up out of your own darkness.

So; how can you possibly make an analysis or decision regarding another and how they are? I don't care if it's a person who just sexually abused ten children and left them in graves. You do not know what you are seeing and how you are distorting it. Let it all be. Do not judge until you know something. You do not know anything because if you did you would nod and say, "Oh great, they got to express their feelings." Both sides agree on every act... always!

❧

You will find that you no longer wish to be at odds within your own self and you are beginning to give up the struggle. The struggle is caused by you needing to be right and to be on top. You will find that part of you does not want to be right and on top. This part wants only to be love. Love and goodness have been distorted for you. You are taught from childhood that to "achieve" is good and to be "best" is good. This is competition; it has nothing to do with goodness. To achieve is very highly rated in your world. If you ran to God with your report card and said, "Look God I got all A's," God would not care. It has nothing to do with being God and it has little to do with healing your universal wounds. If you ran to God with your heart open and said, "Look God I can love and be love," this would very much bring a smile to God's face.

You are not only unable to love and be love; you are also unable to know how to be loving. You think that loving is helping out, pitching in, taking over the responsibility. It is not. Loving is showing how you are and accepting how you are. This acceptance allows you to show you more of yourself and therefore grow into more of yourself. Loving is being kind to you and this, of course, means you are kind to all. It is impossible to be kind to yourself and not allow that to move forward into all areas of creation.

Kindness moves in and around all things. Kindness is part of your very nature. Kindness is how you will one day treat yourself. You will be so kind and loving and generous within your own self that it will seep into all parts of you and take over. Then, after you have been flooded with kindness, it will run off you and move into creation. Then all the world will be seen to be kind. You will literally flood it all with kindness. You will have kindness reports on your TV and radio. It will not be your typical "someone saved a child from an attacker." Instead it will be "Mr. so and so began to grow in love and was good to himself for almost the whole day." This doesn't sound exciting or even interesting to you now but believe me when I say, "It will in the future."

Your level of kindness within is a direct reflection of how much you care for your own self, and how much you care for your own self is a direct reflection of how you will affect all of creation. Believe me when I say your level of kindness to yourself is most important. Stop trying to push you around and stop trying to buy your way out of trouble by jeopardizing who you are. You are not your thought you are the thinker. You create according to what and how you think. You are learning here to be flexible in order to be free. You are not required to be inflexible any longer. You may bend the rules now and you may even bend creation by doing so.

Let yourself out of your prison. You have hidden yourself in a block of cement. Now it is time to come out and bend in the breeze. Let go of your rigid ways. They create stress in an otherwise flexible body. Let go of your need to create rules for yourself and let go of your need to follow rules. Rules are meant for safety's sake. There is no danger. You are spirit; you are not going to lose you. You will always be and your children and loved ones will always be. You are no longer protecting anyone. You have come full circle and you are now cutting off your own nose to spite your face. You are giving out tit-for-tat and it will create what it is. It is not a good idea to give tit-for-tat if you wish to be flexible. Whoever gets in the first blow is in control as you give punishment for deeds done. If you give punishment for deeds done you must believe in evil and in justice. This is not true. Evil does not exist and justice only implies that something is wrong. It is not!

You will find that you no longer will be willing to do your own work. You will discover that God is a great asset and you will discover that God does a good job when it comes to running your life. As you grow closer and closer to God the remnants of all that has separated you will slip away. God will be standing before you and you will be ready to receive that part of you. When you literally accept God, you will be literally accepting the light. All change will then be spontaneous. Your goal will no longer be to receive light as you will have merged with the light. This will be a most profound time for you and you will be filled with truth and love and light. You will abound with loving kindness and you will know no boundaries. You will be "blessed" and it will be the reception of God which has blessed you.

You are in a very precarious part of your journey in that you fear that, upon opening up and letting go of all your past training, you will be putting yourself in further danger and threat. You have always been told to hold on tight to your beliefs and to be strong. Now I tell you to let go of your beliefs and be weak. It is in this weakness that you will find true strength and true power. It is in this weakness that you will learn to grow in light. This strength you have shown is not necessarily a peaceful strength. It has more to do with fear of losing than with the love of being. When you can let go of being the strong one you can become weak enough to allow something else to take over. If you have asked God to take over he will do so when you have your guard down. He will not advance when you are in a strong position and on top. Most of you don't even think about God until you are weak and in need. God is part of you and is totally ignored as are many other parts.

As you begin to see how you are no longer in a position to be the strong one you may actually begin to allow yourself to see God. There are many ways of seeing and experiencing God. God can speak to you, or God can literally touch you, or God can allow you to know he is present. It is not necessary for God to beat you up and put you in chains to do his bidding. You are already beat up and in chains so now God will simply set you free and allow you to enjoy God's company.

It is up to you as to whether you stay or whether you go back to your old beliefs and old ways of being strong and right and on top. As long as you are right you are making someone else wrong. It is not so good as you have been taught and when you learn how this attracts certain energy to you, you will wish to let go of being right. It is far better to have no opinion than to have a fixed opinion. You have all been taught how necessary it is to have a strong point of view and now I am telling you to let go of your opinions and your point of view. You must learn to rise above perspective and this is done through lack of perspective. Do not lock yourself into one way of thinking. You are a non-limited or unlimited being, and you will be free when you let go of your need to be stuck or set in one way of seeing a situation.

Let your God be your guide. Do not seek false gods and do not follow someone else. Be you. Live in you. Trust you. Stay in you and know that God is in you with you. You leave you and you leave God. Stay with God. God is growing in you. Stay at home in you. Do not wish for another body when God is waiting for you in this body. God can transform any body that he is allowed to touch. Allow God to touch you by staying in you. You constantly seek freedom and in doing so you seek to leave your body. You are well aware of this on certain levels. Soon you will be aware of all that you do and how you do it. For now you must trust. Trust all parts of you and they will respond by trusting you. Allow you the same opportunities you would allow anyone who is new to you. Get to know you, then to love you, then to see your beauty.

You will find that not only are you beautiful you are truly illuminated by the light that you so desperately seek. Illumination comes when the light is received and no longer repelled. Every time you say, "that is wrong, this is awful, that is terrible, this can't be accepted," you are repelling the light that is offering to illuminate you.

❧

You are now moving into a dream. You do not so much believe all that I have told you but you have received it well. As you begin to return to reality, or God, it will seem unreal and dreamlike to you. You will feel as though you are moving into a very big dream and it will envelop every area of your current existence. As you begin to move into this dream it will seem to you as though you have lost your attachment to certain things. As you grow and learn you will find that you are not only the one who is creating all that you experience, you are also the one who is putting you into each experience. Once you learn how not to get involved where you do not wish to be you will be learning how not to take on certain roles. Simply because a role is presented does not mean you have to play that role. Simply because the role is there waiting for someone to fill it does not mean you have to jump in. You may choose who you wish to be involved with and how you wish to be. You need not go into a lengthy role and a lengthy relationship to know how you do not wish to be involved.

Once you begin to reenter God space you will be allowed to "see" before you jump in. You will know up front whether you wish to get involved in this or that particular situation. You will know just as surely as you know whether or not you wish to stand in front of a train that is moving at you down the tracks. You will not be so confused as you now seem to be. You will not have to stop and think, "Is this good for me to do." It will simply fall into place if it is meant for you and it will not happen if it is not meant for you. You need not struggle with making decisions that may affect your future. You will be put in situations that are your right place simply because you will have surrendered to God and God will be in the driver's seat.

Now; as you recall I have worked with Liane for some time now. I have guided her and I have moved her. Most of what she has experienced is what you would call awful. She was put into a state of grace when she first began to write for God. Since that time she has left behind a great deal of fear. She not only does not wish to re-experience her past she also did not like the present that I created for her. She was put in her state of grace to keep her happy. If I could keep her happy I could get her to do my will.

So, after she was let free of this state of grace she began to fall into her fears. As with you, her fears were giant and I did want her to face up to who she was. She had a very difficult time as she faced her memories and the fear that was attached to them. She, however, did not quit. She was put into several unusual (for her) circumstances and she was allowed to sink or swim. She did not sink and now she knows this about herself. She was allowed to swim through each circumstance on her own power so she would not count on a God outside of herself to lift her up out of her own fear. As she learned to trust more and more about her own instincts she was allowed to rest and see the gift each lesson presented.

Then it was time to begin to show her how she had created certain rules to keep herself safe from ever feeling terror again. She began to see how she had this need to control her environment so she could feel safe and free of terror. She even began to control her emotions so she would never again betray herself by loving someone who might later do harm to her. She now knows how turned around her life became but, because she was living in her and had no experience living inside anyone else, she considered herself normal and good. She was not and neither are you.

You all have this thing about thinking you're okay, because you don't know anything else. You are afraid to allow certain situations to occur because you are afraid of what may or may not occur surrounding each situation. This is control and prevention. This will soon fade and you will be left with facing the truth and letting go of the fear. For most of you, as with Liane, this entails facing your fears one at a time to allow you to know how you are layered and how you are put together.

If you were to give away your home and your job and any investments you may have, would you be a little nervous? If so you have fear of not being taken care of. If you lost your job and the IRS (or some other source) reclaimed all, absolutely everything that you have, would you be afraid? What would you do? Where would you go? You have little to no money but you do have clothes and a few keepsakes that you sell along the way to buy food. Now you want to work so you can have money to make you feel safe and secure again but you cannot (for whatever reasons) find a job. What would you do? Does this prospect frighten you? You are no longer in charge, or on top, or in control. You have no money – none. Where does your safety come from now? This is the position I put Liane in. I did not do this to be mean, I did this to allow her to overcome her fears and to learn to grow beyond her fears. And she continues to swim and has no intention of drowning in her fear.

This is all for now. Liane hates when I write about her and so I do.

❧

You will find that you are not only the best of all parts of yourself; you are also the worst of all parts. You will automatically become what you believe and you will automatically believe in good and bad. Once you have developed your skill for allowing good and bad to both fade away, you will be more likely to say, "I don't know, do what feels best for you." This will be in response to those who are trying to get you to advise them on any given situation. You, however, will be in a position to see how it does not really matter what choice they make as long as they believe they are guided by their own intuitive abilities. Once everyone begins to develop these skills of intuition it will be much less confusing for everyone.

You will find that as you allow these skills to develop, you will begin to allow people to make their own choices and you will not feel so trapped in your struggle to control others, or to be in charge, or on top, or the one with all the answers. When you begin to let go of the answers you will be headed in a very good direction. You will be going up into 'awareness and understanding' of all elements of creation. You will also be moving into a place where you will relax into the flow of creation rather than bending creation to your will.

You will find that the greater your need for the answers the greater your willingness to shift above any given answer. Your need for answers will guide you to the questions that will ultimately break you free of the need for an exact definite answer. You will once again be in a position to receive out of trust and faith without the need to question why or how or where? As you begin to allow all answers to be nothing more than a possibility, you allow greater possibilities to occur. You allow yourself to be in a position to receive more than just one perspective which allows you to get unstuck. Getting unstuck will put you in the flow and this will put you in the creative force.

Do not allow yourself to stick to anything. Move and enjoy not being tied down or stuck to any one position. Allow yourself to see how the flow works and how, when you are in the flow, it automatically takes you with it and allows you to receive all that is available to the creative flow itself. If you do not jump in the river you do not get to float on it and you do not get to play in it, if you jump in the river you get wet and it becomes part of you by sharing its water with you. So, jump in and get your feet wet. Do not be afraid of the creative flow. It comes to show you how to float free and not sink. You really cannot sink if you are calm and floating. It is almost impossible.

You will find that as you remember who you are you will automatically begin to float free of all that you are not. You are not stuck, you are free flowing essence. Begin to know this and you will begin to see how you need not carry opinions or answers to any given question. You need only have ideas which constantly shift and change into other ideas, and move and flow with the creativeness they have sprung forth from. Your ideas are creative flow in action and they are constantly shifting and changing. Creative flow is creative energy moving through you. You guide it and block it or you may allow it to be. Do not allow yourself to form opinions based on solid fact. Nothing is solid and everything is simply an idea!

⁂

You are among one of the most controversial species to live. You are most controversial in the area of sex. You love it and you hate it. Well, you also love you and hate you but for now I'll address sex. You are very much in love with sex and yet you are so afraid of sex that you put taboos around it. You are not here to taboo anything. I do care how awful and sinful you now believe sex crimes to be. You have blown this whole sex thing way out of proportion. You are not the first species to be afraid of your own reproductive ability. You are, however, the first species to judge themselves as incompetent when it comes to the use of your own bodies. You are so silly! You have totally taken sex away from its natural state. It was never meant to be ruled over by religions or parents or anyone else. Sex was meant to be as natural as sneezing. It was not meant to be controlled. If a child has the ability and the curiosity to have sex at an early age it is due to the fact that that particular child is developed and desiring sexual stimulation. I am talking here about those who experiment early not those who are forced early.

So; if a child is beginning to experiment and enjoy stimulation, that child is ready to learn about sex. Actually, there is nothing to teach. If you were to take two children and leave them to their own design and even place them all alone on a deserted island, they would eventually experiment and learn about sex. It would not be shame-filled sex it would be natural sex with natural curiosity. They would be away from society and its teachings of guilt and shame and they would enjoy sex as it was meant to be enjoyed. No one would say, "You are too young," or, "You do not have the brains to have sex." They would simply research on their own and everything would be quite natural and spontaneous. There would be no sexual guilt and therefore no sexual dis-ease. All would be well.

This is how you once were. You have now restricted sex to the extent that there is not only disease around it there is great abuse around it. It is time to stop the belief in evil around sexual behavior. It is not evil. It is a malfunction that is taking place because the flow of nature has been disrupted. If the natural flow of sex had never been disrupted you would not see sexual misbehavior. You would only see the natural flow of what was meant to be a beautiful gift. Look what you do with the gifts. You are so confused that you fear the gifts and hold on to the fear. You will find that as you begin to unlayer your programming you will no longer require your stringent rules regarding sex or who you have sex with. God does not care how old you are when you first experience sexual behavior. You are not judged for having earlier childhood longings or yearnings or sexual fulfillment. You are not judged by God for any activity you take part in. You are free to forgive yourself and begin to allow the light of awareness to shine on you.

You do not take part in sexual experience out of deviant behavior or evil in your body. You simply respond to energy. Energy moves and you are made up of sexual energy as well as spiritual, and essence. You are more than likely carrying huge amounts of sexual guilt and it is time to release all sexual guilt and allow sex, as well as everything else, to come back into balance. You are not evil beings you are sexual beings. You are spiritual beings and you are God's gift to you. You need not continue to destroy humanity over the belief that humanity is not good enough for God. God is quite pleased with humanity. He gave it to you as his gift. Did you not like his gift? Did it displease you so? Or did you simply not understand the gift and become afraid of it? You fear the most wonderful things and you embrace the most unnecessary. You are truly confused.

You will discover that you do not belong stuck and you do not belong rigid. You will also discover that you are a very big part of God. If you are this big part of God, how can you judge what occurs and how can you punish you or anyone else? Give up this portion of your belief system. Begin to see how you no longer wish to be outside of God. Begin to see how you no longer wish to be stuck. You have been here for a long time and now you are coming out of your shell. You are being born, as a small chick is born free of its egg. You are not exactly a small chick but you get the idea. You have been in a shell. You have been locked up inside your own little world and your own creation. It was meant to protect you and keep you safe. It is not a bad world it is simply being put aside as you grow beyond it.

When you begin to understand the dynamics of all that is taking place at this time you will begin to see how the best thing for you now is to let go and stay calm. Whenever you feel the need to struggle, or argue, or defend, or involve yourself I hope you will remember to "breathe peace and stay calm." This will allow you to get your center back before you get too involved in your exchange with another. All exchanges are energy exchanges and you give up parts of yourself without knowing that you do.

When you begin to learn how energy works you will know how you work. You are energy. You are God force at its best and you are God force in action. You also (in some cases) are God force in retreat. You are not so much coming forward into life as you are moving backward out of life. Many reasons are given for death (as you call it) and many reasons are known for living. One of the main reasons for death is the inadequate supply of energy. Energy received is not high enough to keep you going. By this I do not mean your "get up and go" energy that slows down in old age. By this I am referring to your basic insight and lifeline to God.

As you begin to lose energy it is most important to begin to reconnect with God. What is the first thing you do in a crisis? You reach out to God. "Dear God – help!" is always the first hint of energy loss. You are at a loss and have nowhere else to turn. Now you are learning to turn to God before your energy begins to go. You are learning to ask for help and help yourself. One of the greatest gifts you can give to yourself is the gift of energy. Put your energy into you. Do not put the majority of your energy into projects or opportunities or others. Put the majority of your energy into you and you will be less fragmented and more whole. You will be complete within yourself and you will no longer feel it necessary to run to others to feed your energy. Your energy needs will be fulfilled if you continue to feed you and not give away your valuable life force.

You are so afraid to say "no" to someone in need. You do not know how to 'not' get involved especially with loved ones. You feel an obligation and this obligation creates guilt which will eventually suck you dry. Guilt is a very heavy feeling and it carries you down as it siphons off your much needed energy. You see, in the material world everything requires energy to grow. Fear requires energy to grow as does guilt. You get to choose how you use your energy and most of you siphon off your own and go feed on another to replenish this much needed energy. You do not so much steal it as you make deals for it. "Okay, I'll mow your lawn if you wash my car." You are doing deals as energy exchange. Then your deals get bigger. "Okay, I'll keep your baby and raise it if you will feed and clothe us both." Energy exchange is deal making. Energy has value and is greatly desired by all. There are also much subtler forms of exchange such as "tread lightly around the boss or you will find yourself out on your ear." In this case you all pay homage and give extra energy to the boss to keep him happy so he will not throw you out on your ear.

As you begin to learn more and more about these dynamics of energy exchange, you will begin to see how you put yourself in situations according to how valuable you believe your energy to be. If you placed little value on this energy you may totally give yourself over to another in exchange for your current needs to be met. Some will give up total energy to a lover just to be held and nurtured. It is most important at the moment and so it meets your needs, and you don't care what it costs in the way of energy as you believe your energy is not that important. Your energy is God force. Everyone wants God force. Keep your energy until you are strong enough "in God" to know who you are.

You will soon discover that you are not all that you thought. You have parts to you that no longer function, and you have parts that function quite well and you do not know what they do. You have your own unique way of creating your world and yet you are quite unaware, on your conscious level, that you are creating such worlds. It will be good for you to discover how you create certain worlds or even events for yourself. It will be good for you to see how consciousness creates reality. Consciousness is not only how you see things, it is also how other parts of you see things. If you do not know about the other parts of you, how can you possibly know what makes up your consciousness? How can you begin to know who you are if you do not accept who you are?

As you begin to learn about yourself I wish you to remember that you are hiding you from you. Do not pretend to know all about yourself and your motives, for that type of behavior will only throw you off track. It is best to admit you know nothing and go on from there. You are a discoverer and you are discovering you as you go. As you learn more and more about who you are, you will begin to see how you are not at all what you were taught. You are not plain and you are not inadequate. As a matter of fact you are most adequate in your ability to create. Now we must teach you how to not create certain situations that are no longer necessary.

As it stands right now you create it all. You create absolutely everything that affects you and you create everything that you see. As you judge what you see, you begin to subtly shift that created expression. As you shift the created expression, the creation itself will shift and take on new perspective or simply new meaning for you. Often when you shift the creation by judging it you are allowing yourself to make a choice. "No, I prefer the blue one" is such a choice. You begin to see how the blue brings you pleasure and so you shift your perception to allow blue to be the accepted color for your room. You decide blue will be calming because blue just brought you pleasure. The next time you see blue you may think, "Oh darn, I should have chosen green, the green made me feel alive." It is all just a shift in perception and a shift in feelings.

Your feelings have a very big role in creating any given situation. If you have very big blown-out-of-portion feelings you will create very big blown-out-of-proportion events. If you have less than dynamic feelings you will create less than dynamic events. Some will go crazy over the least little event, others will not be fazed. Often the ones who get overly excited have overly excitable feelings and they are out of balance. Often when you deal with tragedy and chaos you get to see who gets all excited and who stays calm. Often in tragedy those who are accustomed to tragedy will see it as "just one more thing," while those who are not accustomed to tragic behavior will really get excited. This behavior is also reversed in some cases. If someone has been programmed to take a great deal of chaos and abuse they will handle tragedy well because they have been programmed to "take a lot of pain." You then call people, who put their best foot forward under stress, heroes and they can't understand what all the fuss is about. They just did what they have been programmed to do which is to "take a lot without complaining."

Now; when you are programmed to handle tragedy and drama you may find yourself creating a great deal of drama in your life. The part of you that was trained for this is ready to receive more of it. When more does not come this part of you has nothing to do. It's as though part of you is trained in police protection or soldier combat. When the combat isn't needed and no one wants protection, the policeman or soldier in you may go around "looking for" something to protect you against or something to fight for. This is how you keep this part of you alive. You feed it with adventure so it will not turn on you. Now is the time to let go of these drama creating parts of you. Now is the time to create new roles for your various parts. You could have the role of joy giver and the role of peace receiver instead of protector and fighter. Train yourself to act out new roles and to allow your old programmed ones to slip away. It is no longer necessary to put yourself in danger by creating danger.

When you learn to let go of the drama part of you, you will be letting go of a very big creative force in you. You love to create drama because it gets you all excited and makes you feel alive, and you begin to shoot off in all different directions. You are no longer interested in flying off in all directions at once. Now you wish to remain calm so that you might go forward instead of bouncing all over the place. Do not get sidetracked by any fear. It is simply your drama part trying to create a situation whereby you will be out of control and going berserk. You need not fling yourself all over the place to know that you have feelings. Stay calm and breathe peace and do not worry about anything. God is in charge and all is well.

❧

You will begin to see how you no longer belong to fear. You will become so strong in your light that you no longer need fear. As you begin to see how fear has always been in charge, you will begin to allow God to take over. God will protect you in ways you never thought of. You need not hide in your fear and you need not struggle and fight. Simply allow all to be and you will see how God can and will take charge for you. You are no longer in a frame of mind to repel God, so this is a good time to allow God to work in your life. Once you learn how God is you and how, in being who you are, you can allow God to work through you, you will find yourself very pleased with the results. As you begin to find yourself more and more drawn to God you will begin to find yourself in a state of grace. Grace is a natural state of being and it allows you to be only light and love and trust and faith.

Do not fight what is occurring in your life and you will be happy. No resistance please. When you resist or fight against, you create pain. Do not fight against or push against anyone or anything. Allow yourself to flow through each and every situation and do not react or respond to the original action. Allow everything to pass by you and it will eventually land on someone else. Usually you try to block things before they occur and I will tell you now to allow them to occur so they do not manifest into something bigger. Allow everything to be as it is and do not push against it to change. When you find your center you will find it much easier to do this. For now, simply tell yourself that all is in God's hands and you are dealing with this wave coming at you because God is teaching you to swim. It is not coming at you to drown you. It is coming to strengthen your swimming stroke or maybe you can catch this wave and float "on" it rather than swim through it.

Work with energy. All energy flows and can be used in a positive way. You need not hide from what comes at you. You need not run unless you cannot avoid confrontation and struggle. Running is keeping ahead of the wave. It will work at times. You do not require lessons in hiding or running. You do require lessons in floating. None of you are real good at floating through situations. Most of you find them so stressful that you prefer to leave your body and not deal with them. This is when you grab a cigarette or a drink or food, anything that will pacify you while you skip out and leave your body. This is how others gain power over you. You do not wish to stay in body so you give up your body and leave. It is then available for others to use. You may be used by someone who sees where you are vulnerable and goes after your soft spot to get his or her needs met. Often you are an easy mark if you do not like you enough to stay in you and you will have many who feed off of you or get their extra energy from you.

This is all part of the energy exchange game that you play. You will find that, you not only freely give parts of yourself to receive from another; you also freely take what you can get from others. This is give and take as you know it. If you have a car and someone needs a ride, he or she will give something in exchange for the ride. The only problem you now have is that you no longer pay for your rides. You pull out a gun and say, "Take me where I want to go," or you simply steal the car.

Now; all of these games are set up in advance. Why? So you can learn that you do not ever lose. It is impossible to lose. Say that someone steals from you – what do you do? You know it's a game. You know you can create more because you are the creator (writer, producer, etc.) and you know that the universe is an endless supply of energy. So, what do you do? Do you put all of your energy into finding whoever did this and seeking revenge or do you simply make more of what was taken. My suggestion is to make more if it's what you really want. Sometimes it's not what you really want and it's weighing you down in some way, and that's why you sent out the message to, "steal my car – please." Maybe the payments were too big, or you didn't like worrying about such an expensive automobile and how to protect it and keep it insured and safe. It was weighing you down so you decided to ask someone to steal it, only you don't realize you did.

There are many things that you do not realize that you do. One of these is to get others to push your buttons so that you can release built up charge that is also weighing you down and blocking the flow of love and light into you. You must remember to thank the next person who pushes your anger buttons or your fear buttons. That person is answering your call for someone to "please come help me unload some of my garbage."

❧

You are now beginning a journey that will be well known in ages to come. You are creating a doorway for others to follow. This is the journey into love. It is the path to peace and the way into self-awareness. As you continue with your discovery of your own self you will eventually discover how God is you and you are God. This is perhaps the most unique journey you will ever take. It will lead you into God and it will lighten your entire perspective of reality. You will shift drastically in your perception of self as well as you will find yourself most enjoyable to be with. You will no longer feel the need to leave you behind or to get rid of you. You will no longer feel the need to push you around or put you down. You will be so overjoyed at your own existence that you will no longer find fault with you.

You will move into a place of total loving acceptance and you will be well received and well nurtured.

All this will take place as you discover your true identity. As you begin to see how powerful you are and how you create your entire world you will be very careful and gentle with you. Owning you is like owning the most powerful, sensitive, creating machine ever. You are very, very valuable and you have no idea that you are. You have been programmed to believe that you do not matter and you are no more than a human who is here to produce offspring and live the good life. There is so much more.

You are here to signal the coming of God. You are literally the Second Coming and God is literally rising up in you. Do you feel unusual changes and shifts? This is the incubation period. It is when you begin to shift and change and take on light that you are ready. Those who count on an exact moment in history for ascension will be disappointed for it occurs for a very long drawn out period. Ascension is not an overnight event and it does not cover a certain period of time. It is a new way of living and rising above pain and illusion, and it will last until this entire dimension moves up to the next dimensions. It does not occur in a particular year or a certain area of time. It begins and it continues until the job is done.

So; for those of you who are stuck in time and dates and processes... let it go! It is not singular it is plural. It occurs many times in many ways and has nothing to do with reality as you know it now. Do not worry about the timing of such events. When I say "now" this is occurring, or "now" you are ready to do such and such, or "now" you will begin to feel this or that, or "now" is the time for change I do not mean now as today or any day. I mean "now" as far as the information you have taken in and digested. I do not require you to ascend on a specific date. I do, however, know how far you are by how much awareness you have gained and how far you have come in illumination. If you were to pick up these books and read them in one hundred years and saw the dates you may think, "Oh wow, this is old information and it does not apply to me." That would be you limiting your intake of information. Books and information come from a timeless place and therefore contain insights as well as history.

So, do not get stuck in time. Allow everything to apply to you no matter how old or how new. I do not consider you old and unnecessary simply because you have been playing the same old programs for eons. You are valuable and so is information given one hundred years ago. There is much that does not get twisted and distorted and will last into the bright future.

When a single individual discovers these books in 2999 he will be able to achieve the same thing you have achieved by reading them. Enlightenment is not a timed or dated gift. It goes beyond time and it will continue until everything is once again aware that "all is light." So, do not worry that everyone does not make it back to God. God has a perfect plan and it lasts forever and is always with God. God does not teach as men would teach and there are many very valid reasons for this.

So, for now, allow God to show you how beautiful you are and it will allow you to become all that you are, which in turn allows God to rise up in you. You are each at this place and you will find that as you clear your subconscious debris you will also be allowing more light to enter you. The bigger you grow in light, the lighter you become and the higher you rise. Your vibration is much quicker and so you literally begin to ascend. You will do things that you have never dreamed possible only because you were not told that they were possible. If you can imagine it you can create it! Thought creates and what is held in your consciousness becomes your reality. Allow your thoughts to be kind and loving. Love yourself so that you might love your creation. You are the one and only creator of your creation. Ask for God to create for you and God will.

⚬

You will begin to experience the most remarkable shifts in your awareness when you begin to get in touch with all parts of you. You will find that simply knowing how you tick is a tremendous opening to your own awareness. You will begin to see how you block your own good and how you create pain and stress for yourself. You will be allowed to see how each part of you has a job to do and each part of you is working very hard at its job. How did you create these parts to perform certain roles? You began by allowing fear to rule. You said, "Okay, if I am going to be attacked I need defense." So you built a defense team within you that now goes crazy and will do whatever is necessary if you believe you are in danger and require assistance. The biggest problem is that you no longer know or recognize danger. Your defensive team is inside of you and it is trained to defend, so if anything moves it may get attacked before it has the opportunity to attack.

This is how you protect you. Some of you are even aware that you are overly protective or just very defensive. These parts of you who play this role take their job very seriously and they have gotten punchy and out of control. When you are constantly on guard it is very difficult to not get tense and tight and irrational. The part of you that plays "defense" for you is out of control. I suggest that you talk to this part of you and ask them to no longer defend you. You no longer require defense of this sort. Now what you require is love and understanding. You are tight and tense from all these years of protecting and defending; now it is time to allow God to take care of your fears. Turn your fears over to God and allow God to show you how your fear is simply an illusion.

An illusion is not real. If you were a child feeling threatened I would walk with you through your fears and allow you to see how they were made up and unfounded. You can allow God to walk with you through your fears also. You can allow God to show you the truth. The truth is that you are looking so hard to find a villain that you are creating villains. Why would you look for villains? It is to appease your defensive team that lives within you. You must feed them energy to keep them alive or they will take energy from you. This is how you drain your own energy. You keep your defenses up for so long that you grow weak and exhausted.

So now this team has been discovered working in you and is a part of you. How will you continue to feed them? They must eat or die. How about you begin to feed them trust and faith? This is a very good diet for such a big strong team. They may wish to take on the role of doling out trust and faith. It's a full time job, as is defense, and the rewards are far greater. The next time you communicate with your defensive team I suggest you offer them a new job. Make it a change to a higher position; they will understand such an explanation. Oh! You don't communicate with the defense workers in you...? Well I suggest you do. They are taking over and taking control of your life. I would think that you would meet with them daily on the running of your life. You have here an opportunity for growth. Go within and discuss your defense in regards to trust and faith for a trade on arguing and defensive action. I think the energy group that is working in you to defend you will gladly trade in their boxing gloves and guns for some harp music and fun.

You will soon discover that you not only do not know your own parts, you also do not know how to use your parts. You are like a machine that came without instructions and no one has ever taught you to see into your own self to know what is there. As you begin to learn how you have many parts to you, you will begin to see how it is time to know what these parts are for. Do they do service, and if so, do they require maintenance? If these parts require maintenance, where does it come from? How do they survive and how do they draw energy to keep going?

It would be a very good idea to know what is going on inside of you if you are going to live inside of you. Don't you want to know who is in you and how you work? Don't you want to know why you are so afraid and what makes you afraid? Don't you want to know why you are not whole and happy and well and in peace and joy? No. Most of you do not care. You simply want a quick fix — "Give me a pill and make it go away." Well, this time it is not going away with a pill. It has outgrown medicine and it is taking over. There is no quick fix and there is no pill that will shut it off.

It is fear! Fear has settled in and taken over. Fear does not care how old you are, or how strong you are, or how young you are, or how tall you are, or even if you are a tiny baby. Fear needs energy to grow and fear is feeding off of energy. Whose energy? Anyone who will donate. How do you donate? Look at your life and you will see. It is stress, anxiety, pain, illness, boredom; it is all part of fear.

Fear causes greater fear simply by multiplying itself. Like a cell that splits and divides it splits and grows into more and it is your greatest disease. You are afraid of everything including your own mind, your own body and your own soul. How can you possibly grow in love when you are so dedicated to fear? – "Do not do this it's bad. Do not say that it's wrong. Do not cuss, do not spit, do not hit, do not talk without permission, do not be yourself. Do not listen to bad music it will harm you. Do not watch bad shows – it will harm you." You are afraid to listen, to look at, and to be you. You are totally afraid of everything and anything because you do not understand your own working and who and what you are.

This will all change! You are going to become enlightened about you and how you work. You are not going to fear you any longer because you are going to look at you. You are only afraid of what you do not understand and what you do not understand is all of you. You are totally in the dark about you. You do not want anyone to probe too deeply into you so you do not acknowledge what you carry. You do not want to go too deeply into you because you basically believe that you are evil. You know what thoughts you have had and how twisted they seem to you at times. You know how you have this rage that turns to anger or just righteous indignation. You know how you hide things from others so they will not see your true identity. You do not want them to know how awful you are for they will surely leave you.

I will tell you now that you all carry all of this. You are not alone. It is the unspoken law that you do not speak of such things. It is the unspoken law that you use everything in your power to keep certain parts of you under control and do not discuss them. It is unspoken law that you quietly suffer in your confusion and pain. After all, "Only crazy people need analysis and only weak people cannot control their own feelings of rage." This is untrue. You are all out of control and most of you are turning your rage into self righteousness and disappointment. You are disappointed in friends, in life, and in yourself.

Well, it is time to look at the problem and it lies right inside of you. You will learn to turn your rage into quiet understanding. In doing so, you will no longer feel disappointment nor will you feel angry. You will also drop the righteous act. Once you begin to quietly go within you and work with your own rage you will begin to heal. Your stress will disappear and your irritable side will no longer exist. You will be comfortable living "in" you and, therefore, you will be comfortable living in the world. You are now at a big turning point and you may continue to ignore the problems that lie within you and continue to tag others for the blame, or you may get real honest with yourself and say, "Okay, I'm doing this somehow so let's look in me and see how."

You will find that once you work in you to fix what is out of balance, you will be very happy that you have finally come home to you and found your source. You spend so much time focusing outside of you that all of your energy goes where your focus goes. If you begin to focus inside of you, you will be sending energy into you. You will begin to grow with your own energy. You will begin to heal with your own energy. You are complete within yourself if you will just pay attention to yourself. You give your attention away to everyone and everything but you. You are a wealth of information right inside. You are valuable and you do not know it. You are like an undiscovered gold mine and you merely want to ignore you and focus on everyone and everything around you. It is like playing with the images in your mirror. Come back to reality. Come home to you!

✦

You will begin to see how you not only do not know you; you also do not wish to know you. You have an aversion to you. You are now learning to love and accept you and, in order to do so, you must at least learn to look at you and know what is in you and at work in you. You are all so afraid to "look at thy self." You have no problem figuring out everyone else's life and telling them how to fix it but you refuse to "look at thy self." This is self reluctance and self-denial. No one denies you except you. No one dislikes you except you and no one is afraid of you except you. You create all that you see (regarding those who will not accept you) by not accepting your own self. You create those who leave you by leaving your own self.

You are not in love with you. I can barely get you to sit still long enough to discuss you. You want bigger, more exciting topics. "Give us something more interesting," you shout. Well, this is it. This is about the most interesting I can get. "Bring it all home to you" is all that is left. You are the creator! Look what you have created. How does it feel? If you do not like it look right within yourself. It has absolutely nothing to do with anyone outside of you. You create it all. Whether you create out of judgment, or fear, or love, or hate, or revenge is totally up to you.

So; what do you use to create? How do you know what you use to create? How can you change what does not feel so good and take responsibility for what you create? How will you know what you are creating for tomorrow? How will you know it will be better than yesterday? Or do you crave for more of the same? Do you like what you have created for yourself? Is it joy and bliss and peace? Do you see joy and bliss and peace, or do you see war and violence and pollution and fighting and pressure, constant pressure to perform? Well, I suggest you get to know you because you are in charge and you are creating out of control. You are like a parent whose offspring has grown into a serial killer and now you disown him. He is not what you desire in a son so you have turned your back on him and you deny that he is part of you. You are denying you and you are cutting you off from love by allowing you to continue to ignore you.

Go back to you. Learn to love you and to accept all parts of you. Ask God to intervene and to show you the way. Ask God to enter you and to take control. Do not be afraid to live in you. Do not be afraid to confront all parts of you. Do not be afraid of the vastness of you. Take it one step at a time. Enter you. Love you. Be you. Stay in you. Give you the breath of life by being at home in you. You spend so much of your time out of you and now I want you to return. Return to you so that God may be in you. You are gallivanting all over the universe and you spend very little time in you. This is what kills you (as you know you). This is what drives the body to death. Lack of love kills you. You are the love. You are the God force. You are the creator.

Stay where you live. You live in you; you do not live in your neighbor or in your neighbor's business. You live in you and in your own business. Why do you find you so unworthy and so boring? Or is it simply that you cannot bear to face you and know you? What keeps you so interested in figuring out everyone else when you are the one who needs help the most? What is it that drives you into the lives of others? How is it that you would rather give your attention (your energy) to others? Give your attention and your energy to you. Trust me when I say that "You need your own light for you." You are growing dim and it is time to reignite yourself and grow into God.

৯৬৯

*F*or as long as you have been in body you have not been in control. You do not know the full extent of the use of your body and you have no idea how often you are in or out of your body. You are all moving all the time. You come, you go, you attach, you unattach. When you can learn to stay in you, you will be learning to be fully your true self. You will know how you work in you and you will know how you work outside of you. You will find that once you have left your body you do not realize that you have. You are so accustomed to being "here and there" that you do not realize that you could stay home and remain centered. You travel and you zing around and for you it is the natural state. You do not see how you are causing yourself to lose parts to the unconscious. If you could stay in body while you do your creating you could consciously know that you are the creator.

If you were to begin to watch your energy level shift and change, you would see how it is a gauge and would show you how often you are in you. Your being "in" has a direct reflection on how much juice you receive. It will show you how much energy is being given directly to you. It will show you how much you nurture and give to you. As you learn to see these shifts in energy level, you will learn to know your own inner workings. You will begin to realize how much you need you to survive. It is not only your own energy that you need it is also your own guidance and your own wisdom. As you begin to see how you are being taught by you as you grow, you will gain a whole new respect for you. You will no longer view your identity as simply an ego. You will begin to see how you are a great deal more and how valuable you are to the workings of your daily life.

Once you begin to see how you are creating everything that occurs, you will be capable of understanding that you do not know much on a conscious level. As you begin to learn how you create absolutely everything for a reason, you will begin to wonder at the reasons for this or that and how those reasons may be good and actually affect you in a very positive way. Once you begin to understand the workings of your own ideas for the process of creating, you will see how you are not only creating to stimulate growth you are also creating to grow.

As you grow you create from new levels and as you create from new levels you stimulate growth. It is a constant process. It is life pushing you up a ladder one step at a time. You get a jolt of stimulus to force you to raise your foot and leg to the next step, and then you get another jolt to force your foot down on the next rung of the ladder. This process is then repeated as you take step after step up the ladder, and all you do is complain about the jolts because you only feel like you are being pushed at, and you are. You will, however, begin to see the benefits of this type of growth. It is how you create. You put it out there and then you bring it in. You contract and expand. You breathe out and you breathe in. Do not be offended by the jolts. You are sending them into you to create growth. Stimulus creates movement and you are moving up!

You will begin to know you as you have never before. You have emotions buried in you that are working against you. Once you learn to allow your emotions to move and to release, you will be allowing creative energy to move and to release. Whatever you hold in is working at creating for you or against you. Say that you have emotionally charged energy in you that says you are guilty of being bad, how does this energy stay alive in you? It must be fed in order to live and what it lives off of is your ability to believe in good and bad. You must believe you are bad in order for it to survive. It will create whatever it needs to survive, and its survival depends on you believing you did something wrong or you will do something wrong. You need not create anything for it will create for you. It is part of you and it is energy.

As you begin to learn how to use your energy wisely, you will once again see the benefit of being free to love and forgive yourself. You will find that you are no longer in a position of pain once you have begun to let go of your need for pain. Your need for pain is fed by your desire to keep you under control so that you will not run amuck and do what you have in the past. And what is it that you have done in the past that requires such strict restraint? Why, of course, you murdered and beheaded and skinned-alive people. You did all sorts of objectionable things and part of you remembers. You have a past that goes back millions of years. You were not born yesterday you only think you were.

So; when you begin to get the urge to let go and free your soul, another part of you will step forward and remind you of your atrocities. You did not kill out of love; you killed out of fear and out of reaction to fear. You did not kill out of wisdom, you killed out of ignorance. You are no longer as ignorant as you once were. Some are returning to this state of unknown consequences, but, for the most part, you know how this responding and reacting does not work. Violence begets more of the same while peace begets more of the same.

When you wish to let go of the part of you who creates violence, you must allow it to show itself to you and do not judge it. It is you and it will change and play a new role if you only ask. It is not stuck in its role; it is only doing what it was once told by you to do. So, if you find a violent part of you moving to the surface request that part to play a new role. Forgiving would be a good reversal for this part and it would really stretch the ability of this part. Ask this part of you who has been playing tough guy to play the forgiving one. It will be a most enjoyable switch for him after so many years of being violent. It will also allow him to become more loving toward himself for all that he has done in the past. He will begin to see how to forgive himself for past offenses just by looking at forgiveness as a role. This will allow you to be forgiven, which will allow you to move on and no longer be held back by past deeds.

You have been around since the beginning of time and you have done many things that you are not yet aware of. You will learn to forgive you by allowing everyone the opportunity of forgiveness. If you cannot forgive them it is only because you are stuck in your own un-forgiveness and your own need to punish you. Give it time. All healing comes with one step at a time. One more jolt to get that next step up to the next rung of the ladder. You will come to a point where you are actually thankful for the jolts. This is awakening and realizing the benefits of living and moving out of pain.

❧

You will begin to feel as though you have not ever known you. You will feel as though parts of you are totally in charge and you can only hold on for the ride. This is how it has always been but now you are learning that it is. You are learning how to love you and to know you and this entails all parts of you. You have the part that wants to love you and you have the part that wants to hate you. You have the part that wants to forgive you and you have the part that wants to hold judgment against you for all your sins.

When you learn to let go of these parts of you, you will find life will be rewarding indeed. When you have learned to retrain and re-teach and re-educate your parts, you will find that they are most anxious to work for you in any capacity you require. After all, they have always done your bidding only you didn't know they existed and that you controlled them. Now they are ready to continue to do your bidding and they will feed off of whatever you give them. Give them love and they will feed from it and create more of the same. Give them fear and you will continue, as you have, to create worlds full of hatred and violence.

You are beginning to see how you are the creator. If you think you want to get back at someone – that very thought "get back" becomes a part of you and it is the sign that you flash to others. That sign says "Hit me because I believe in being hit when you are bad." It also says, "Hit me because I am going to hit you if you turn on me so you might as well hit me before I hit you." This type of communication creates your reality for you. You get to be a victim of your own belief system.

No one ever gets hurt by your thoughts except the thinker and mover of thoughts and that is you. You move them into place to do the work for you and then you cannot understand why your life is not working. Your life is not working because you believe in an eye for an eye, and because you are a criminal (in your own judgment) you get to be punished; and it starts by you accusing you and it ends with you passing judgment and wanting to get even and asking for pain for whatever crime was committed. When you believe that the only way to get a bad person to react in a good way is to punish them or give them pain, you automatically become what you believe. You now get punishment or pain for every little thing that you do that is considered bad or wrong.

You do not know who you are nor do you realize the extent of your emotional trauma. Please let go of your need for punishment and you will feel better. You will know when you have let go of this need, for you will no longer feel it necessary to straighten anyone out or make them see the "error of their way." There is only "belief" in error. Error does not, and never has, existed. It is an illusion.

Error is not something bad, it is you not knowing or understanding your own pain and confusion and so you label things as good or bad; "This is bad it will hurt me," or "This is good it will make me feel better." You take drugs to feel better and you drink to feel better and you pop a pill to stop the pain. Put it all away. Let go of the need for pain and it will leave. It will have nothing to feed on and it will die. It is not so much that you want pain, you are just so into it that you do not know how to come out of it. Stop the belief that if you give enough pain and punishment to someone they will change and be good. This is control at its greatest. This is taking over the body and the mind of another. You have enough to take care of right here "in" you. Stay out of others. You do not belong in control of others. Look at the job you have done with you. How can you possibly think you should control another?

For now I will leave you with this thought. You are not who you think you are, so how can you possibly know who anyone else is?

~

You are very much a part of you and since you are, you can no longer ignore you. You are the one who is in control of everything and you are the one who does not care if you get what you desperately want. You are the one who blocks your own progress and you are the one who does not allow you to receive. You are blocking reception in order to block pain. You put up your blocks to receive all that you get because what you were getting did not feel good. You began to give your power over to the part of you who would keep your pain to a minimum. This part of you protects you at all costs, and this part of you also reacts like a receptor to block messages and distort messages. It picks up signals and gives you false information.

This is done out of a need for protection. If you were once harmed and it had a dramatic effect on you, you may find that you have a distorted view of the world. This view comes from distortion out of a need to protect. You will be shown danger where there is no danger. You will find your nervous system going crazy and your receptors out of control when you land in certain situations. You will find that not only is there nothing to be alarmed about, there is also nothing to harm you in the particular situation. You only "feel like" you are in danger. Your receptors go crazy and begin to send signals that put up your protective barrier, and you get confused and upset and "feel like" you are going to be harmed or lose something. Then, just to prove you right, you allow something to be perceived as harmful or as loss so you can justify your dysfunctioning alarm system.

This is similar to a child's overactive imagination. You get to move into a new situation and right away you see all the problems. This will make change very difficult for you. You will constantly find something wrong in every situation and every job and every mate. You will not know how to see the good and the positive because your payoff is to find the harm; the bad, the negative, the problem. If you spend your entire life looking for danger because you were once in great danger, be it in past life or in this life, you will find danger in even the safest situation. You are programmed to protect you from harm and, in many cases, this protection has become attack. You now are so defensive that you lash out at others because you believe they are a threat to you. You hear what they say and some part of you translates it into danger. No one is saying what you are hearing. You are making a meaning out of nothing.

In most cases, after you have decided that this is so or that is so, you will react to the person or the situation from the perspective you believe them to be coming from and they will, of course, begin to respond as you are expecting, simply because they are reacting to you reacting. You each react and respond without thinking and it is time to stop. It is as though one strikes out and slaps your face so you slap back, so they slug back, so you kick back, so they draw a knife, so you pull your gun, so they blow you up or set your house on fire. Stop responding. You are all trying to get everyone to realize how awful their actions are when, in actuality, you are the one who is twisting everything to mean what it is not.

You do not need to take part in this type of response. Do not be drawn in. Let it go right past you. Do not jump on someone else's case and do not jump on someone else's words. Let it all go by you. It is their response to you. You are responding so they respond. If you do not hit back it will end. They will go find the appropriate response or "attention" they are looking for. It is no fun to kick a pillow or argue with a pillow. Why do you think you do not argue or fight with your pillow? It will not fight back. It will take what you give and it will not respond. If you do not wish to get hurt do not "engage" in hurtful activity. Do not push another's fear buttons just to show them how you have power over them. Do not play these games. It is not necessary to scream and yell to get attention. You do not need that much attention. If you will simply "breathe peace" you will create your own peaceful place where you can have all the energy you require.

You do not need to get attention from another if you are loving you. You will automatically know you have all that you need just by being with you. You do not require the approval of someone outside of yourself and they do not require your approval. You are not in them, you are in you and you are not guiding them you are guiding you. Get your own life in order and you will no longer find yourself in your neighbor's business. You are so full of shame and hatred for the self that you cannot even stay "in you" or "in your life," so you go get your nose all bent out of shape over your neighbor's life. And why wouldn't you? After all, you've pretty much given up on you and decided to go live for everyone else. It's easier than staying in you because you find you so disgusting.

You can tell just how disgusting you find you by how often you find yourself figuring out everyone else's problems instead of your own. Don't come from a perspective of, "Well, he does this so I do that," come from a perspective of, "I wonder why I find this or that so distasteful? I wonder why I react like this or like that. I wonder why I can't see peace instead of struggle. I wonder why I can't see love instead of fear." When you begin to ask the right questions you will begin to see your answers. Until then you will continue to go in circles.

☙❧

You will find that you are not only unaware of your own creative abilities you are also unaware of your own destructive abilities. You have often wondered why you do not have pleasure and joy and pure bliss. It is due to the fact that you are now in a state of constant pain as a result of punishment for sins. Whether these sins are in the future or present or past, you are so into punishment that you begin to find fault and to start your righteous behavior which creates the required punishment. When you begin to learn how to allow your creative flow, without the need to block it and control it, you will let go of the need to create boundaries and limitations. This need for boundaries and limitations was created by you to protect you from your own creative force. You are protecting you from God. You push you away from God and you do not know that you do.

Every time that you judge something as bad or awful or terrible you judge God as bad or awful or terrible. If you cannot accept creation you cannot accept the creator. You are stuck in a position that condemns and you do not know how to stop condemning. You are condemning your own self with every unjust thought you think. Everything you think comes back to you. You operate within you and your energy flows within you. Your thoughts flow in you, your thoughts do not flow in your neighbor. You may not know this, but you are shooting an arrow into you every time you think that someone is stupid, or ignorant, or offensive, or not as understanding as you. Do not get trapped in this judgment roll. Let it go. Simply know that God is at work in each and every individual and know that God will heal he, or she, when he, or she, is ready. It is none of your concern.

You focus on everyone else and I can't get you to begin to give attention to your own self. Please start to notice you. Please begin to watch how you act and react. Please begin to take good care of you by running good thoughts through your body. Please begin to forgive you by running forgiveness through your body. Please begin to love you by running love through your body.

Please pay attention to you. You are the light of your entire world. Everything that you see is in you. You are the cause and the effect. You start and end in you. You begin to rise above struggle by seeing peace, and you see peace by letting go of your need for reparation. You are killing your life force by forcing you to suffer because you believe that you are right and life has treated you unfairly. You are not right and right is not might. Right is only ego misplaced, and what you are is God, and God is not might God is light and love.

❧

*W*e will begin to see big changes when we begin to walk into ourselves. The path into the self is indeed dark. It has not been lighted until now. You light the path into you by showing yourself what is in you and how you use what is in you. You begin to see how you are not only not what you thought you were, you are also not who you thought you were. You are a very rare species and you do not know that you are growing and evolving in such rapid terms. You are using your own genetic and biological codes to unravel your own secrets. You are discovering you for the first time ever and you are now on the road to knowing who you are.

As you change and transform and develop, you will begin to see how you no longer find it necessary to indulge in trivial behavior. Trivial behavior is a lot of "reacting" to situations. You put all of your energy into reacting instead of simply flowing and being who you are. Do not react and respond. Begin to see how you react and what the signs are. Look for your response in any given situation where your buttons are pushed and begin to see how much energy you put out after they have been pushed. This is responding to the threat or the discord of another. Someone gets all riled up and decides to take it out on someone or something. You happen to be handy so you get the blast of energy. What do you do with that? Do you pass it on and continue to blast others, or do you sit and feel bad and awful about yourself and what has just occurred? Do you begin to get angry and turn the blast inward, or do you slough off this blast and allow it to pass on through you?

Knowing you I am sure you have figured out how you do not let it pass. You get all involved and hurt and upset, and you complain and talk about it and get all these hurt feelings out of the way. You are not exactly allowing things to flow yet, but at least you are catching on a little bit as to how you block your own flow. Your energy will block up in you when you internalize a blast, and it will build if you do not allow it to simply roll off of you. You will find that you not only do not allow things to just roll off of you or past you, you take them in and digest them.

You are devouring your own inner need for energy by eating up what is said to you out of anger and discharge by another. Do not get involved. Do not eat it. It is not yours. Do not be so ready to be defensive, as it is blocking everything. Defense is not what is needed. What is needed is a little trust in who you are, so when someone blasts you it does not tear you down. You can only be put down if you believe you are not good in the first place. A person is drawn to you (when you do not support and believe in yourself) to show you who you are. In this case it is someone who does not believe in him or herself.

Be kind to you. Know you well enough to realize that you are not bad and nothing that will be said to you will ever offend you. You cannot be put down by anyone but you. If you do not already believe that you are bad, you will never feel bad after someone has criticized you, and you will never be angry at the voice of criticism. It is all you showing you how you "react." Stop reacting and begin to know who you are. You are not here to get all wrapped up in possible emotional systems. You are here to flow and move with the current. You are just passing through and you do not know yet why, but you will very soon. Keep up the good work. You are discovering more of you on a daily basis... this is good!

⁂

You are going to see how you are not only becoming one of the most entertaining species you are also becoming well known. You are well known for your stubbornness and for your need to be right. You are also well known for your inadequate intake of light. Each and every time that you deny light you close down a little more. This causes a greater anxiety and a greater feeling of inadequacy.

Most often you do not realize that you are denying light. You believe that you are simply being you. You are not. As a matter-of-fact, you have lost your identity and become something that is not you. You changed to come into this dimension and now you must change to get back out. You may wish to know that it is your circle of desire that continues to bring you in. You have "desire" to return and "desire" to have your needs met and even "desire" to do it right. Let go of the need to do it right. Begin to see how you cannot do it wrong. You are no longer in a position to be wrong. You are only being, and evolving, and transforming and it is not wrong. Nothing you can ever do is wrong. You do not begin to rise above this dimension and then call it wrong. It is not wrong to rise up. It is not wrong to dive deeper. It is simply a matter of choice.

You are now beginning to know how you are, and in learning about how you are I do not expect you to criticize yourself more. I do however, expect you to begin to see the light and move toward it. You are not moving out of you, you are actually moving very deeply "into" you. You are moving into where the pain and confusion lie. Why? So that you might learn to express your pain and confusion in order to release it. You have been pulled into your own self in order to view yourself and release those trapped parts of yourself. You get drawn "into" you by constantly and repeatedly talking you through and into you. Thought moves and consciousness follows thought. If I can get your thoughts moving in a new direction I can easily get you to become aware. Consciousness will follow the direction of your thoughts. You are becoming conscious and aware of parts of you that you did not know were in you. I turn your attention into you and you begin to send consciousness into you. This wakes "you" up.

You are in a very peculiar phase as you are looking at danger and defense. This gets tricky because you wish to defend your right to be you to the very end, and what I want is for you to "give up" the right to be you. You are no longer going to be you, you are turning yourself over to God which means that you give over your ego identity and become whole and part of "all that is." You will remain stubborn for some time in this area. It will take more work than any other but I wanted to let you know where we are in this path into you; this turning-in process that is showing you to yourself. To know you is to accept you. To accept you is to love you and to accept and love you is to accept and love the world, for you are the world and everything that it contains is in you.

∿

You will learn that not only do you begin to see how you create; you also will see how you step in and interrupt what another has been creating for his or her own self. This is especially true if you believe that his or her creation may affect you in some way. If you live with someone who creates chaos or disruptive behavior, and you are constantly interfering and making things run more smoothly, you automatically create a smoother reflection for them to see and they never do get the "results" of their creation; and, therefore, do not "realize" what they are creating. Allow creation to work and allow yourself to work within your own aura or energy field. Allow yourself the insight that will lead you to your own karmic pattern by allowing yourself the insight that is right inside of you. You carry a wealth of information "in" you and it is time to begin to unveil it and to use your power with consciousness and with honesty to your own self.

You will find that as you begin to get yourself unraveled you will see more and more how you "act out" what you do not release. You will wish to learn to release energy from within so that you do not explode or "act out" your energy. Say that you have been collecting stress all week at work. Your stress grows and grows and shifts to anxiety and then drops into anger and resentment. Now it will begin to create for you. You may slip and fall, or you may get put in your place by the boss, or you may get a big headache, or you may lose your favorite ring. Whatever is "just punishment" and pain for the amount of revenge that is now built up from the stored anger.

So; why don't you help the anger "out" of you? You may do this by picking up a pillow and beating your bed to a pulp! Maybe your bed is not the culprit or the one you are angry with, but you will get your "get even" fix and you will move your anger up to the surface. This is how you "consciously" disburse and dispel built up anger so you will not create a negative force that is directed at someone else but comes from you so therefore affects you. You are creating darkness by not dealing directly with your own darkness. Begin to look at your dark energy so that you might shed some "light" on it. It cannot continue to be subversive if you continue to be "aware" of it.

When you become aware of how you "create" your reality you will know that you no longer need to create pain. You may live pain-free, and you may defuse your anger and need for pain until you can learn to come off the karmic wheel that you have created for yourself. You need not continue to create pain and punishment. "Act out" what you create so that you may see it grow less or grow more. You are the creator. You are the source. You allow or you stifle. You create! Become aware of how often you do not wish to see how you are doing and you will know your anger level. You will know how angry you are at you by how little you wish to look at your own stuff, and how often you wish to look at and into everyone else's workings. You are learning avoidance of yourself and what you avoid is what you will never get to know. Knowing you is loving you. Allow you to love you by knowing you.

❧

You are not the only one to have a problem listening to your inner workings. You have the ability to hear and to be all that you are. As you learn to listen you will learn that you do not require so much a new body as you require education for this body. You all lack education. You were never taught how to get back to the basics of your nature. When you are young you are led away from natural instinct and intuitive ability. You are told how "everything you now know and do is wrong and you require discipline." You are believed to be ignorant and out of control, and yet you are closer to your true nature in childhood than you are at any other time. But this soon changes as you grow accustomed to pleasing your parents and teachers and educators.

You are not so much a product of your environment as you are a product of your very own special training. Each individual was trained and taught how to relate to others and how to interact with others. As you get closer and closer to death you get tired of interacting by the rules and begin to spend more and more time alone. You just don't have the energy to interact, and this is due to the fact that your interaction was based on you winning and you being right. You no longer feel the need to win and be right but you feel the need for attention. However, your need for attention was always based on you being right and good. So now your only means of gaining attention is to be good. This is why many elderly people become very set in morality. They no longer have the energy to compete which is interaction so they become "good" which is morally correct.

As you begin to see how you are creating roles for yourself you will begin to see how you all compete for attention. When you learn that it is not necessary to be seen or heard you will have learned to let go of this earth plane. Desire for attention will keep you focused here. Desire for God will keep you focused elsewhere. This is how you create and this is how you live in this dimension. When your desire shifts you will shift. You will move from being right, or good, or great, or wonderful, or nice, or smart, or intelligent, or beautiful, or handsome, or rich, or powerful to being God. This will be a very big shift for you. Right now you are all focused on what you can attain, as this is what you are being told that creation is. This is far from the definition of creation but, for now, you will play where you are. You will find that as you learn to let go of more and more of your old definitions of what is what, you will be redefining your own self and your own focus within this realm.

You are not dumb and you do not require re-education. What you require is the ability to see the whole picture. You have this ability and you are moving up your ladder of awareness. You too will learn to look above any given situation to see what is really going on. When you learn to look above, you focus above the situation which keeps you from slipping into the situation. "Keep your eyes on God and your hearts on love."

You will learn to know God by getting to know you and you will learn to know you by allowing you to be, without judging you or putting you down. Every time you hold judgment the weight makes you drop to your knees. This too is good. Without this humbling experience you would never raise your eyes up to God and say, "Please help!" You would only pray at designated times and give your list of demands. You truly "look to God" when you are humbled. Humbling is very good and yet you judge it so. But this too has a purpose, and each time you judge your situation you will find yourself creating more of what you are judging. Like creates like. Get up out of the muck and the mire of your own judgment. Judge everything as love and light and allow everything to have a very good purpose!

❧

As I began to walk along the path to enlightenment I began to see how I no longer wished to be so afraid. I began to see the shadows for what they were and I began to see my soul as the light that was casting my shadow. I could see how I could not only 'not' become a light being without casting shadows, I could also not become God without seeing evil. I could not become light without the dark and I could not become God without the devil. I came to understand that all truth is a lie. All light is dark and all God is evil. You may take anything in creation and twist it until you call it something else. You may take all energy and make it move to your tune. You get to call the shots so you get to name it light or dark. You get to call it good or evil and you get to see how you have responded to your creation of good and evil.

167

It is all you. It has always been all you and now you are beginning to see how you do it. You create it all and then you get to call it whatever you want to call it. You may decide to call it love, or you may decide to call it ignorance, or you may decide to call it hatred, or you may decide to call it darkness. How do you know what to call it? Who taught you what is good or what is bad for you? How far back does it go? How long must you walk this path before you find that place where it all began?

You are very much a part of all that you create and so you have created yourself with full knowledge of your own ignorance and evil. You do not carry more evil than you see in the world. You look through your eyes and you decide how much is evil, and the amount of distrust and upset you have for the world outside of you is the amount of distrust and upset you carry within. You are not evil you only think you are. There are no evil acts, you only think there are. Stop calling you evil and you will stop seeing everyone else as evil. You are creating evil by naming it as evil. It is not. Stop creating evil. Let it go. Give up this need to create horror and allow everything to simply exist.

Allow everything to be what it is. What it is is energy. Stop being so ridiculous as to call energy bad or evil. Begin to allow it all to be. Live and let live. Do not judge your neighbor for it is you that you judge. Do not talk stink about life as it is your creation that you are calling stinky. You live in what you create. Do you want to live in a stinky creation? No. You do not. Give it a rest. See only good in all that you look upon. There is good in absolutely every situation.

I will now give you an example: once upon a time a little girl sat down to write books for God. How is it that she tapped this source within her? Well, she had great pain and confusion because she did not love herself, because she was taught self-loathing and abuse at a very young age. She began to experience tremendous trauma at age five and so she shut off her love and her feelings until she was so lonely that she literally screamed for God to intervene.

So, how did she begin to hear God? Her need was so great because she was in so much pain. Who assisted in creating so much pain? It was a soul who loved her so much that when she asked him to be her father he quickly replied, "Will it be a big job?" And she answered, "Yes." He then declined as he knows how roles are played out on earth. She then begged and pushed and prodded until she talked him into this role of sexual abuse or incest. It is not that it was necessary; it's just that she wanted to *release* big karma and get off the karmic wheel. So she decided to engage the efforts of a soul who she believed she owed big time from past lives. She said, "You can get back this life and you don't even have to kill me." He, of course, was not so sure he wanted to get involved, but she was a very persistent talker.

So, now we have her talking him into playing this painful role and, of course, she had to put something in the deal for him as well. You see, she can't be the only one to benefit from this deal. So now we have our volunteer and he will do his best to play out this incest role to the fullest, but it will not be easy for either of them. Energy is very strongly judged on earth and both of these souls are well aware of this fact. It's like diving into a gray soup that is thick and gets into your eyes so you do not see. It even blocks your pores and stunts your senses.

So, now we have our volunteer and he does his best to violate all the rules of propriety that are in place concerning children and adult behavior towards them. It was not an easy role to play and he has a great deal of guilt and self-loathing as does she. But, she now has God and her books. She got what she ultimately wanted and it is now his turn to receive for his efforts. It is not as you believe. We do not play that, "He will get his just desserts, God will punish him for his sins," game. There is no punishment, there are only rewards. God loves and does not intervene unless you allow him to and, even then, he does not play by your rules. God is love and God is light, you are all playing a game that is going to end soon and you too will be love and light. No evil. No get backs. No judgment. No punishment. Ahhh! What a wonderful world it will be....

꧁꧂

You will begin to discover how you are not only very much alone inside of you; you are actually not inside most of the time. You spend so much time focusing everywhere else that the inside of you is neglected. Of course, this accounts for a great deal of illness and garbage that goes inside of you. You really don't care because you are not "in there" and so you allow yourself to ingest whatever suits your purpose at the moment. It's not until later, after a large build up of ingested material, that you begin to feel unwell or ill at ease, and then you must look "in there" at what you have done to the inside of you.

Still that does not stop you. You go to your doctor and say, "Fix me in there," and he says, "If you do not stop smoking or drinking or eating that you will die" and you say, "Fix me in there," and so he does his best. But now something is beginning to change. The doctors are beginning to say, "We don't know how to fix you in there, but we are working on it." This is causing even greater feelings of loneliness, because now you see how you could have taken better care of you but didn't. You could have loved you but didn't. You could have liked you enough to stop poisoning you but you didn't. You are killing you "in there" and you don't care because most of the time you are not "in" there. You will find, however, that most often you are learning a lesson. You may get it this time or you may return and do it all over again.

If you want off the karmic wheel, I highly suggest that you stop killing yourself every time you get a new body. You are building up greater and greater guilt for yourself to overcome. I tell you to not beat up another so you will not judge you and build up guilt, and now I am telling you to not beat up you or you will have built up more guilt and judgment. Leave you alone. Stop poisoning your own inner organs. They have a life, a job and a purpose. No smoking, no drinking alcohol and no chemicals of any kind go into you. If I were to tell you that you now have a new machine that will take you to paradise and it was most important to take good care of this machine and clean it daily would you? If you would – if you want paradise that much, you will begin to see the wisdom of keeping the machine in tip top shape.

Of course, you seem to care more about machines than you do your own body. Could it be that you have projected your energy into machines like cars and boats and even houses and this is why you care so little about your own inner workings? Are you so busy at work figuring it all out that you have no time to spend "inside of you?" Could it be that your attention is focused on everyone else and everything else, and you have no attention left for you? Could it be that you are going to die from lack of love and lack of attention because you do not want the responsibility of owning you? Could it be that you find it much more interesting to look at other people's behavior and other people's mistakes? This is a sure sign that you do not wish to look at your own self. If you cannot spend time with you, you cannot know you. If you cannot know you, you cannot see what you are doing to the "inside of you." You are not in a very healthy body. You must learn to love you and to care for you. Stop poisoning you and start loving you.

*W*hen you begin to see how you no longer belong in fear you will begin to see how you belong in love. You must learn to love you in order to become all that you currently are becoming. I know that this sounds like redundant talk to you but it is most important that you love you. You will find that you get very bored discussing you and your habits because you do not like being told what to do, and you do not like being told that you do not have all the answers, and you do not like being made to feel about four years old.

You want to believe that you are sophisticated and talented and above average intelligence when it comes to experience and life. After all, with all that you have experienced one would think that you would have learned a lot. You did. You learned how to behave in public. You learned how to use table manners (if you were taught) and you learned how to please others so they would not be annoyed at you and maybe hit you. In some cases you even used this information as a weapon and learned how to displease others so they would not feel as though they had complete control over you.

Now you are in a big body and your mind is still filled with small behavior. You react to situations and you do not know why you do. Oh, you "think" you have all the answers, but I tell you here and now that what you "think" is only part of another story that is now affecting your judgment and causing you painful interference. When you were four or five and you wanted to bug someone you simply did not "obey." Now you are past four or five and you are having a very hard time with this thing called "obey." It is often the cause of many problems.

Some of you think that you are so smart that others should simply drop their beliefs and listen to you or "obey" you. Others of you think you do not know enough regarding life and so you blindly "obey." Still others feel obligated to "obey" the rules, or the boss, or the king, or whoever plays the one in charge. It is causing pain and confusion and it is also causing problems for those who wish to rise above this entire dimension. It is very strong in parents and children. Parents always thought they should be in charge. Now they are seeing how their children will run away at the least provocation.

This is a time to learn and to understand. It is not a time to condemn one or the other. You are all trying on roles and "acting out," you are all beginning to see how tiring these roles can become. When you learn that you are "behavior trained" you will begin to see how it is not just the one who pushes your buttons who has a problem, it is you who has a problem. You are only drawing someone to push your buttons so that you might grow beyond your problem. Your problem is behavioral training. You have been trained to behave defensively since you were born. You are not small and defenseless anymore and it is time to retrain your behavior. You need not give another person the power over you to push your buttons. The way to see it differently is to come from love. If the person is truly dangerous to your health I suggest you leave. Do not stay where you are getting hit or harmed in any way. Leave! If the person who pushes your buttons is not physically threatening to you I suggest you begin to look for the light in that individual. Once you see the light you will be able to see more than fear.

Often, when you are in your own fear, it becomes impossible to see anything but fear. It is like being in a big cloud of smoke and you can see nothing but smoke. Wait until the smoke (fear) clears and then look for the light in the other person. If you cannot find a light I suggest you move to another situation where you will be with those you can easily see the light in. This is not to be taken to mean that an individual may not have light. It simply means that if you cannot find the light in them you will never be able to heal and grow with this individual. Allow yourself the space to be with those who love you and accept you and truly care for you as you do. When you are seeing love in others it will assist you in seeing love in yourself.

Now; when you begin to move away from those who do not love you, you will find yourself wanting to create a big scene. Do not. Allow everything to evolve and to move gradually and naturally. If you simply stomp out the door with your self-righteous behavior you will be creating a disturbance in the energy flow. Allow everything to flow gradually and gracefully. There is a grace to everything... even creation. You have been programmed to believe that to leave another is bad; dreadful, sad, awful, tragic, tearful. It is not. It is evolution. It is just as normal and natural as meeting or coming together. It is not bad to leave; to separate. It is good. Move on when it is time. Do not commit if it does not feel good. Commitment is such a big deal with you people. Give it a rest. It is natural to move and shift and grow, be that with a mate or on your own, it is up to you. Do not hook up to someone else's wagon if you are not headed in the same direction.

You will begin to learn how you hook up to feel safe and end up feeling drained and unsafe. You cannot place your eggs in someone else's basket and expect them to still be your eggs. Your eggs belong in your basket and you all try to make someone else take responsibility for certain parts of you. Keep you! Keep all of you and allow others to do the same. Stop feeding one another's insecurities and neurosis and addictions and behavioral disabilities. You are all playing this very unhealthy game and it is time to just stop and begin to focus only on you and what you need to do. Let everyone else heal their own wounds. You do not have time to because you will be far too busy once you have seen how big your own are.

You will begin to see how you no longer wish to remain without your own loving self. This part of you is the part that will grow to care for and nurture you, and you will begin to see how you no longer belong to the fear and unwanted feelings that go with fear. You are in a position to begin to "know thyself," and as you begin to look inward towards your new home I wish you congratulations on moving in. As much as you "pay attention" to business or to loved ones you will now learn to give to your own self. You will learn to ride into you and to know that you do not belong outside of you. The way to heal you is to bring you back into you. If you focus your attention on you, you will begin to grow in you because you are moving your focus into you, and therefore shifting the energy from outside to inside. You are no longer being put in a position of scattered energy, you are being put in a position of centered energy and its center will be right inside of you.

As you begin to know more and more about your own self and how you function, you will begin to see how you are not only 'not' going to learn how to live with you, you are also not going to learn how to live with your thoughts. This is, of course, if you do not begin to accept "this you" in order to transform "this you." Here's the deal – you can't change what you don't own and you can't change anyone but you. Oh yes, you may think you have had an effect on changing someone, but you have only been a trigger, or an incidental spoke in a wheel of events that the individual drew to his or her own self in order to change and grow. Well, now you can own you and change you. You can become all that you ever wanted by allowing you to own you. You then begin to accept what you are, and then you begin to allow yourself the space to grow into you and to transform what is no longer necessary into something more productive.

As you begin to see how very accomplished you can become at transforming various parts of you, you will find that you not only do not wish to leave you out, you also do not wish to be left out. You will begin to rise above most of your own fears when you can get back to you long enough to know you and love you and assist you in this rise up. You are going to discover how you are not only 'not' one of the most admired (in your eyes) you are actually one of the most disliked. This, of course, creates great controversy at a time when you are searching for peace. You are not only 'not' the one who lives in you; you are also not the one who loves you. So, you may create some struggle as your self-hatred begins to face off with your self-acceptance. You will find that these two clash hard when they do begin to push for reign over you. You may find yourself looking at parts of you (or feelings) that are quite strong and quite defiant.

Once you begin to work with these parts of you, you will find that you are learning balance in order to bring everything into your center. Your center is the healing place and it will allow you to heal all of your unhealed parts. It will also allow you to heal new parts that are constantly growing and developing. For the most part, you will find your center near your heart and you will feel safe if you project your feelings from this center. You will also begin to know that you are not so bad and no one is really that concerned with hurting you. It is all you beginning to wake up to feelings of mistrust in order to form new feelings based in trust.

You will find that as you grow "in" trust, you will be forced to let go of mistrust. Mistrust is very frightening when it comes to the surface. You may feel overwhelmed and even get paranoid over something that you believe is dangerous and harmful. Mistrust is a very big, powerful energy force and it is especially strong in those who have great childhood pain from controlling individuals who were unkind. You get hurt when you are small and you begin to build big walls of protection so that you will never allow anyone to harm you again. Now is the time to release this mistrust and allow the pain to surface, and begin to replace the wall of pain with a wall of love and acceptance.

You are now moving into acceptance and with it will come love and kindness. You will begin to see you for the loving entity that you are and you will begin to know that you never did do anything wrong. You only thought you did and you thought you were punished. Do not believe this. It was not punishment it was ignorance, and you did no wrong you were simply experiencing pain so you could learn to come out of pain. You have a great deal to learn and you will not learn it from the rules of your society. You must begin to know you in order to raise you above ignorance and into "illumination."

❧

You will begin to know that you do not own you when you begin to see how you treat you. You let yourself go unattended for days at a time while you travel out of you and exert your energy elsewhere. Keep your energy on you. Keep your focus on you. Keep your attention on you.

Do not try to distract your feelings and emotions. Go into them and learn who you are.

Your emotions will catch up with you if you continue to run from them. Your emotions do not wish to be ignored and are looking for release. Your emotions are not so much being put off as they are being stuffed in and ignored. Your emotional body is ready to explode and will soon require a very big cleansing if you are to balance. Your emotional body cannot balance without your permission. Emotions that are held in are thought to be dangerous, or frightening, or too awful to express. When you learn to hold in emotions you will be learning to hold in you. You will not be expressing you and you will not be releasing energy that was meant to flow through the emotional body.

You are learning now that you are not only body you are energy. This energy that makes you up is very powerful stuff. If bottled, it could easily blow up a building. It is not necessary to blow things up, but if you as a species do not find release soon you will blow yourselves up from your own trapped and blocked and suppressed energy. You will simply explode if you do not learn how to use energy wisely. So, I suggest you begin to look at your "blocks." What makes you terribly upset and why? How do you justify your being upset and make it okay to continue with this "act" you put on? How is it affecting you and how does it affect your life? Is there a pattern? Do you always repeat the same role? Do you want to change it? Can you learn how to unlimit yourself in this particular area?

These are all questions that you should ask yourself when your buttons are being pushed. It does not matter so much who is pushing your buttons as it matters that *you* created those buttons for a reason. Why did you create such sensitive areas "in" you? How can you learn to balance these areas? And how can you learn to release your own built up charge without using this button pushing game?

So, as you begin to look into you and your inner workings I want you to remember that you created these buttons to keep you safe from something, and that something is dead and gone a long time ago. In some cases it is dead and gone lifetimes ago. You will find that the more you travel into you to discover you, the greater will be your ability to see how and where you are fooling yourself. You are not only 'not' being honest with yourself; you don't even begin to know yourself. You are only protecting you from danger but now it has become much more. It has gotten out of control and is ready to burst inside of you like a tumor. It is not so much a part of you as it is energy that is trapped and stuck in you.

You are now beginning to create a new sense of life and how you wish to exist as part of life. If you continue to deny the existence of certain feelings they will simply come up and hit you when you least expect it. Do you have problems controlling your emotions? This is due to the fact that you are backed up and damned up with rage. Yes – you. Dear sweet little you are just full to your ears with rage and turmoil that is bubbling and boiling and waiting for release. I do suggest you begin to let go of some of your pent up energy so that you may balance.

I know that exercise is good for you to release this pent-up energy but it has grown to such proportions that you need greater release. Beating up a stuffed animal is very good. Also hitting a bed with your fists or kicking a pillow until you are exhausted, these will all assist in releasing pent-up energy that is aggressive and hostile from all these years (and often lifetimes) of built-in tension. You are beginning to rise and to do so you must "let go and let God" take you up. This energy is meant to anchor you and hold you back. It is based on the illusion of fear and danger. God is now in charge, and fear and danger do not exist where God is. You are learning to become God. This is how you become God. You simply let God be and allow everything to flow or move to its right place.

You will find that the more you release, the lighter you become. You will let go of so much "charge" that you will visibly relax and feel the tension leave your body. Your poor body has held on for so long, to so much programming, that it is stuffed to the rafters with old programs and old files of misinformation. You will find that when you begin to clear the body of all this old programming, it will begin to operate much more efficiently and it will begin to thrive on its new diet of love and care and kindness. You will want to stay at home in you and you will no longer feel the urge to abandon you for days at a time.

❦

You will begin to see how you are not only made up of a series of old outdated programs, you are also made up of a series of signals and nerve sensors. When you enter a situation that is not conducive to your makeup you will be put into an on-alert status. This will be all of your signals going off and telling you that you are in danger or something is amiss. At those times try to remember that God is taking charge in your life and he will take care of everything. You need not figure out the best way to respond, or react, simply because there is no best way.

When energy begins to "discharge" the best thing to do is to stay calm and try to get out of the way as the energy flies at you. This can be done in several ways. One is to be your own self and walk into your own drama, or the second way is to be God and back out of the drama. Backing out is usually best. It allows you to be you while you let the others play out their roles. Do not try to stop a bully from being a bully, but do not allow yourself to be playing the bully/victim game.

It is best to know that you no longer wish to play these games and to remember that you are rising above such triviality. Begin to see how God would look at each and every situation. Would God get involved or would he simply try to keep peace and enjoy his day. It is not necessary to explain to an individual how awful they are. It is also not necessary to point out their faults or to point out their attributes. You have gotten so accustomed to building people up that you praise them when you do not understand how this creates separation. You will learn in time but, for now, I wish you to be who you are in all situations and who you are is God. If you can't figure out how to act in any given situation "act like God" until you can "be God again."

You will find that the majority of you do not even begin to know how unlimited you truly are. You may begin to see yourself as a piece of gold with unlimited value or you may continue to see yourself as a dirty ol' rock. It's up to you. You get to decide who and what you are and you even decide how you will treat you. Do not believe that you have so little value. You are God and God is gloriously brilliant and you too may be gloriously brilliant. This is how you will know you when you come face to face with you. You will shine so brilliantly that you block out everything but your own light. This will be independence day and it will feel very, very good to you.

You will begin to see how you create an illusion just by convincing yourself that something is occurring. This does not necessarily mean that you are seeing correctly, but you usually "respond" to what you think you see and what you think you see becomes your reality. You begin by knowing that you are feeling something and then responding to that feeling. The only problem is that most of you do not trust what you cannot describe. If it feels odd to you, you simply mask it as something else, something that you know or can understand. If you encounter a new feeling that is particularly strange you may even consider it to be useless or nonexistent, when in reality this new feeling has a great deal to show you.

As you learn to distinguish between fear and loneliness, a pattern will emerge for you. You may discover that you are lonely out of fear, or you may discover that you are afraid because you are lonely. You might find that you do not wish to be alone or you might discover that you only want to be alone. You are simply separating yourself and learning to be one. When you have discovered the singleness of your existence you will no longer wish to be you. You will then seek God. As you learn to unravel the various layers that have covered you to keep you hidden and playing this game of hidden emotions, you will begin to know how to be your own true self. You will begin to know how to reign as a deity instead of a pauper. You will know how to be love with total acceptance of self and all knowledge of self.

You are mostly learning to be free. This requires freeing you of certain parts of you. You will find that you no longer require the need to hide certain parts of you as you will be free to set free these unnecessary parts. They are mostly you but they are also illusion based on past life and other situations. They no longer apply and they are disrupting this part of you and pushing into this life. Do not be afraid to face those who killed you or maimed you in the past. These parts who were injured are trying to show you how dangerous certain individuals may have been in past lives. These parts that are coming forward into this life are very much in control of things and it is time to move them away from you and into their own dimension.

No one crosses over dimensions without a reason, and a lot of what is occurring right now has to do with redemption. Everyone who has been harmed in the past will push to get your attention so they may move to the light with you. These are not all you. Some are confused and others are trying desperately to get you to remember them so that you will take them forward with you.

It is not often that dimensions are crossed but it does occur. When this occurs simply allow the parts who are shaking you up to settle back down and then begin to ask them to move out of you. You need not carry the fears of past you's and you need not require others to carry these you's either. It is best to allow them to integrate and take on a new role in the light of love or to move on to their next location. Do not carry what you are moving out of. You are leaving it behind for a reason and you do not wish to be taken down any longer. You are now moving up not down. You are now being light and sharing the love of self. This is not what some will wish you to do. Those parts of you from past life and those parts of you who do not wish to go up will struggle to keep you down. This will create struggle and confusion and even greater fear because *you* do not see or know all of you. You don't know what is going on or how many you's there are, so how can you possibly understand when you are feeling put upon by un-describable parts of the self?

You are walking a fine line here in that you know who you are but you do not know most of who you are. The part that you know is so tiny compared to the part of you that is not known to you. So many things occur without your awareness and they all affect you. You are the one who feels. You are the one who has the nerve endings and you are the one who is in you. You are the one who projects forward and you are the driver of your own car. You are not aware of all the workings within your car but you drive it anyway. When others begin to run into you, you do the best you can to swerve around them and keep your car headed in one direction. Sometimes these other you's will literally take the wheel for a while and they are so strong that they will convince you that it is all you making your choices as usual. It is not. Certain parts of you are strong enough to push their way into the driver's seat and take control. This is why it is a good idea to let God drive for a while. If you can just "trust in God" to get you home you will be okay. Let go of your need to control and let God control.

You learn to take control of your life from the time that you enter earth. This is part of what you are taught as part of earth school. You learn to know how to use your body to walk, and to talk, and to eat, and to think, and to figure things out. Not everything that you have been taught beyond those needs has great validity but that is a whole different issue. So, as you learn to walk and talk and eat, you also learn to listen and rest and be still. In the quietness is where you will find the truth. At those moments when your mind has stopped its chattering you will find your answers. You will also find God in you at those times. It is not all that difficult to get to peace if you know how to shut it all off and stay calm. It will help you to know that you are not always chattering in your head. When you sleep you pay attention to what is going on and you see differently. You even know more when you are sleeping. You reconnect to the part of you who is supreme and you do not frighten so easily.

You are not much of a fighter when you sleep either. As a matter of fact you really are quite nice to be around when you are sleeping. Oh, a few of you get far too noisy but other than that you are very peaceful beings when you sleep. Maybe you should all sleep more. Have you ever thought of that? Maybe the whole world is simply tired and cranky and needs a very long sleep, just like sleeping beauty. You wake up one day after being kissed and you are in love. Yes, this is a very good idea. Take a nap children. Take lots of naps and rest up for the coming kiss.

※

When you begin to see how you no longer wish to be all caught up in your own emotional dramas you will begin to release your hold on emotional pressure. You put pressure on you to perform in a certain manner and you put pressure on you to be a certain way. Once you begin to see how it is no longer important to make an impression on any specific person, or group of people, you will begin to lighten up. You are moving very quickly into a position of not knowing what is important and what is not. This is due to the fact that you are letting go of your need for perfection or your need to be the best. You will be much easier on you when you no longer require specific action to make you suitable. You will find that you are not only suitable just as you are, you are also very much in you when you can accept you just as you are.

Now, when you begin to see how you are creating certain situations in your life you will begin to know how you will find your own areas of weakness. What you believe to be a weakness in your character may not be a weakness but a strength. And the opposite is also true, what you believe to be a strength in your character may be simply a weakness. You have no way of knowing as you no longer have control of you, and you have not for some time. You only think you do.

In actuality you are governed by your nervous system which sends and receives impulses from the part of you that is "in charge," this part of you lives in your mind and is called fear. As you begin to let go of fear you will begin to see great changes in your support system. These changes will come in the way of neurological impulses which will automatically tell you that you are in good hands and headed in the right direction. You will no longer require guidance from outside of yourself and you will no longer require direction from anyone but you.

You are fast becoming an idling fool in the eyes of some, but in the eyes of God you are becoming God and you are transforming. God cannot work through someone who is too busy to stop and allow God time. Be idle. Do not allow your need for specific behavior to push you into activity when you may "be still and know God." It is most important to learn to know who you are and it requires no running around and no putting on airs and no pretending to be more than what you are. It simply requires being in you. It requires your consciousness to rest in you. It requires your heart to be at peace within you. You are the center of you and you are all that is required to know you. It is no complex task. It is very simple and very basic and very easy to love you by being you. You simply stay focused "in" you and rest "in" you. Do you know how to "be" in you and do you know how to "rest" in you?

You will find it difficult to begin to settle into you when you first begin. Your focus will shift back outside of you because you are so accustomed to being out of you. As you learn to stay in, you will learn to be more at home and more relaxed and more at ease. The more of you that is in you the more comfortable you will become, the more confident you will be about your future and the more secure you will feel. It's almost like the feeling you get when you have millions of dollars in the bank and you don't owe anyone anything. You will have you in you and you will not have parts of you going out to everyone else. You will have all of your gold "in" you. You will not be stretched from one end of the country to the next. You will be right inside of you where you belong. All of you will have gathered within you to give you full power to be you. You will no longer be scattered and you will no longer be looking for you in everyone you meet. You will have drawn you back to you by the simple act of wanting you to return. You will have packed up all parts of you and brought them home.

Now, for the first time, you will be whole. You will be no part of anyone else and they will be no part of you. You will be "one" within your own self. This is how you become "one." You do not go out and join hands and circle the globe and say, "Okay, now we are one." You must become one "within" before you will ever see this reflection without. The outside world is creation. You are creator. You and God are one. You *will* reflect this onto creation, but for now it is up to you to get home to you. You belong inside of you. Stay focused on you. You are not living outside of you because it is fun. You are living outside of you out of fear of returning. You believe you were pushed out. You must return in order to be you. You are God. Please come home to God. Be in you. Stay in you. Focus your thoughts on your inner being as much as possible. It is so hard to get you to project into you. You are so busy projecting into everyone else. This will calm down once you begin to trust you enough to let you in. Then the walls of defense will stop attacking anything that wants to get close and they will allow you to enter.

You see, not only have you kept everyone else at a distance by your mistrust, you have kept you at a distance also. This is not difficult to correct, but it will take a little time as all parts of you begin to feel free enough and safe enough to return to you. You are made up of many layers and many parts and they will all integrate as you grow into yourself. This is the miracle of birth. This is God being born to man. This is heaven come to earth. This is the big "shift" in consciousness. You are coming into you. God is entering you. You are God and God is you. You are being born for the very first time and it will feel very good once all the trauma and fear have disappeared. You will like being born into heaven. It is what you have been waiting for since time began.

∾🌿∾

You are now in a position to be of service to your own growth. You may begin to "know thy own self" by asking certain questions like, do I really hate this or does it remind me of something that once hurt me? Am I really in pain or am I struggling with a future projection – something that I am afraid will happen in my future? Do I really love me or do I simply want me to be right and win? Do I really want to be best or do I want to continue as I always have and receive recognition for it? Am I really hurting myself or is it something else? Do I want to rise up or do I want to be a better (morality) person? Do I think I am God or do I think I am gaining on this whole game of life? Do I wish to be God or do I simply wish to win?

Power is a very interesting energy and it may be used to bend others to your will or it may be used to create. It is not so much how you gain your power as it is how you use your power. Do you lord it over others by your superior attitude or do you spread joy and joyful attitude? Do you rise to the top and not progress alone or do you rise to the top all on your own? It's up to you how you will rise up. It is not up to anyone else. You are free to choose how you will learn to use your power. Once power is attained it is very easy to reverse its pull and go in the opposite direction.

You are learning now how to gain power simply by knowing what makes you tick. You can begin to know what makes you tick by asking yourself how you make yourself angry and why? Why would you choose anger instead of joy? How is it that you began to use anger to control yourself and others? Is it perhaps the energy impact that anger carries? Anger has a very big impact on everyone around it because it is so much a part of everyone. But – what about joy? What kind of an impact can joy have? Well, I will tell you now that joy will set you free. Joy will make you shift gears and see a whole new perspective. Joy will also allow you to flow through life without getting stuck to fear. Joy will allow you to be flexible and joy will allow you to remember.

When you are in anger you tend to forget big chunks of you. When you are in joy you tend to remember who you are and how you are. Choose joy over anger in any given situation and you will have risen ten thousand fold in your energy shift. You will have doubled and tripled your power source as you will have come from joy. Joy is a simple state of preoccupied bliss. Bliss comes from deep within you and may be released into small doses of joy until you can handle larger doses. This will be similar to taking a drug when it first begins to occur for you. You must learn to ease into joy as it has become an unnatural state of being since you switched over to fear.

Once you begin to experience joy it will be difficult to stop. You will want it all the time, but you may not know how to process joy so take it easy until you come into balance. You still have many things at work in you and to experience joy is to excite some of your old programming. Did you ever wonder why you get what you want and then destroy it? You are coming from negative/positive and each can cancel out the other.

Now; here is the catch. When you no longer believe in a world of good vs. bad you can have it all. One will no longer cancel out the other. They will come into balance and work together. This simply means that when you get a huge dose of good you do not require a huge dose of bad to balance. You no longer have bad in your life because you have made everything to be "okay" instead of two parallel dualities of good and bad. Now you have one line running through you that says, "This is good and will serve me but I choose this instead." Everything becomes a choice instead of a punishment. It now is a river of options and you can choose one without another part of you canceling it out. This becomes more and more free as you become more and more free of creating good or bad.

Leave everything in the middle. Do not create it and it will not exist.

Now; when you begin to receive from this well that is omnipotent you will be receiving from both the left hand and the right hand of God. You will know the strength and the weakness and everything in between. You will know the energy that flows through you and you will choose out of clarity and not out of ignorance of your own inner workings. You are the best of the best and you need not struggle to be better. You need only "look" at you and in you and see the power you have within you to create anything you wish.

This power has always been here and you have simply not known how to turn on your switch. Some have discovered how to create great power but this is usually short lived and then it is canceled in another area. One area of a man's life may be so high while another is so low. This is not balance it is checks and balances. You have worked from this system of up-and-down/back-and-forth for long enough. Now what is required is a steady stream "up." Do not confuse this with only (what you call) good. This is all good. Productive good has come out of many things and you can still receive great joy as you learn and grow. This does not have to be the school of hard knocks; it can simply be the school of higher awareness and evolution.

So, as you begin to experience joy, do take it easy and don't rush into anything. You have many parts at work in you and old patterns and habits die hard. It is time, however, to begin to choose joy over anger in any given situation. So, if someone yells at you be joyful. If your anger comes up and you have to beat a pillow to express your anger do so and do it with great joy. You may express any emotion and do so joyfully. It will feel very good for you to put a little glee and giggle back into your lives. Do it with joy. Do it all with joy.

~❧~

You will begin to see just how you have grown when you begin to see how to let go. The biggest problem in letting go comes from not wanting to be hurt. You are so afraid of being hurt that you do not want to turn your safety over to God. You are afraid that no one will take good care of you and you now believe that God does not really care. After all, he let you get in this mess so why would he lift a finger to help you now. Well, God does care. God has always wanted to assist you but you refuse to *allow* God to assist. You continually expect to do things your way and not allow God to do things his way. It is part of duality. You expect to be put in God's care and you expect to be put in danger.

When you begin to learn the difference between danger and lessons you will have begun to learn a great deal. *You* want lessons. You would not be here if you did not wish to learn. Once you learn a lesson and evolve a bit you look back and think, "Great, look how much I've learned." But while you are in your lesson you are upset and confused and, in some cases, in pain. This is due to the fact that you contain upset, confusion and pain. A lesson is presented to project the pain and confusion and upset right up and out of you. It is a way of relieving your own self of built up garbage. So, as you begin to face new lessons do not be upset and confused. Just allow everything to pass. You already know what will pass as you are well aware by now that you contain explosive amounts of anger and hurt and revenge. So, when someone or something triggers you stay home and simply watch your garbage pass. It is like doing your enema. Maybe there is cramping for a moment and then everything passes out of you. There is sometimes a "holding on" period. But this too passes.

As you learn to simply watch your lessons come and go you will see how you no longer create your world according to the level of garbage that you are expelling. You will begin to relieve yourself of unwanted debris and you will literally see it leave you. There is no need to get involved with it as it goes. Simply watch and learn and listen.

As these eliminations take place you will become aware of how you have created your reality in the past by confusing what is leaving with what is coming into your life. One must leave for another to enter, but you have never been very good at letting the one go in order to receive the other. You prefer to hold on to everything until you literally explode with holding everything in you. As you begin to let go of one to receive another, things will begin to move smoothly in your life. You will be able to allow energy to flow through you and to allow yourself to become a conduit of energy. You will become the distributor of your own energy by simply allowing things to flow in and out of your life. If you try to trap it all in your life you will have a very big deposit of built up energy as you now have.

This energy needs release. The damned up feelings are overriding everything else and they are creating rage. You are raging on the inside like a bubbling volcano that is ready to blow. Once a volcano blows we have meltdown and lots of destruction. Do not blow! Defuse yourself a little at a time. Use your triggers. Be thankful for those experiences that trigger you. They are a very big gift at this time and they will assist you in defusing your own built up energy. It is backed up in you and requires release. Sit back, stay as calm as possible and let your triggers do their job. They are your gift. Let them work for you.

Know you. Know what you are doing. Know that lessons are presented to assist not to harm. Know that you are not in harm or danger except right inside of you. *You* are the dangerous one so you see the world as dangerous. It is all you. Your own ticking bomb is frightening you and blocking out any sense of true reality. You must defuse you. A trigger is a gift. If you get your buttons pushed go quietly to a private place and begin immediately to release. Scream in your car, or stick a towel in your mouth and scream in a private room. Do not upset the neighbors or involve your co-workers please. If screaming does not get it out, beat up your bed and kick and stomp on your pillow. It is time to throw a fit and be a child again. Release the angry child in you who is so afraid and so frustrated.

This will work! It is energy build-up and charge. If you do not release it constructively you will hurt someone, or break something, or get in a fight. Usually, the one who gets hurt in the end is you. You always charge through your emotions like a bull in a china shop and you don't think about anything but freedom from your situation. You are panicked when your buttons have been pushed and I want to bring you back to a calm "awareness" of what you are doing. You may walk calmly to your room and begin to beat up your bed until you feel release. This is your lesson for today. If you do not choose to fight you may choose to scream at the top of your lungs. Scream out your rage and do it in private. A car is a good place for this. You can roll up your windows and drive away from traffic and scream until it is all out – especially if you have always repressed your verbal expression of displeasure. You need to clear the energy that blocks your vocal cords so you do not bring throat problems.

Now, once you have begun to beat up things do not worry that you will transfer to beating up real people. You will not. You are simply releasing built up charge before it gets so big that you turn into a killer or abuser. Yes, we all have it in us to kill and we have all done so in the past. For now we will simply kill off our pillows. It's a lot easier to do and it creates less confusion and pain. This is your lesson for today. Not all lessons have to do with penance. Some are actually fun.

⚜

You are among the most unusual of a group of angels who are coming home. You began by leaving your space to allow for a build-up of energy that would bring you down into three-dimensional reality. It is very difficult to carry all knowledge and all wisdom and then to pretend to know nothing and hear nothing and see nothing. You are now learning to hear and see and know and look at everything differently. As you learn to transform your beingness into what you are now becoming, you will have learned how to become whole once again. You will have full working capacity of all parts and you will have the ability to know that you are working and living on many levels at once.

You will see how you are not only one of a host of angels who is regaining its senses; you will also see how you are regaining big chunks of you that were left behind until you could accommodate their energy. You are waking up to many of your abilities and powers and, as you do so, you will be taught how to handle your knowledge and you will be guided about your development. Do not worry if you think you are becoming overly sensitive because you are. You are beginning to "feel" things that you ignored in your slumber and you are beginning to realize how you don't have to get all upset over every little thing you "feel."

You will begin to balance out and you will begin to shift into even higher gears of awareness and perception.

It's sort of like being Superman. Someone lies to Superman and he tunes into the "thought" of the lying one to determine the truth. You will begin to tune into thoughts and feelings and this will confuse you for awhile. You will wish to know that everyone lies for whatever reasons, so don't waste your time and energy trying to prove how they are lying. What you are learning here is to see through situations so you no longer create so much confusion for yourself.

If you begin to find yourself involved in playing good guy/bad guy please stop. Your job is not to rip someone else's lie apart. Your job is simply to *evolve*, and if you spend all of your time ripping everyone's lies apart you will be stuck in this game forever. It is none of your business, you are just passing through. Let them live how they see fit and you get on with the job of passing through.

Now; when you begin to experience periods of telepathic awareness, do not make a big deal about it. A good student does not boast because he knows that anything can and does change at any given moment. So don't get too hung up on anything that is occurring at any one moment. As you begin to move and shift you may begin to feel a little uneasy about your own stability. You may begin to feel inferior because you do not recognize what everyone else seems to recognize. You are seeing the world differently and this may cause some confusion so it is not necessary to create greater confusion by pushing what you see onto others. You are just learning to *accept* what you see and to push it at others will only set you back.

When you begin to recognize those who are at your level you will begin to feel very connected. It is sort of like a big convention for cooks. They get to swap recipes and tell cooking stories and feel camaraderie. This type of connection makes you feel good because it gives you confidence that you are not alone in what you do. As you begin to evolve at different speeds, you may no longer have common ground. You may find that you feel like you are all alone in how you see things. This too is good. You will learn that not everything is done in groups. Groups are for safety and you are moving out of safety. Society chose long ago to move in groups in order to have power and you will find that in a group it takes a little longer to evolve because what the "group" thinks is what counts, where as, you may think way ahead of the group and need to evolve individually. This group thing can also work for you. If you are a less evolved thinker, the group power can project you forward more quickly, but the group will usually stop anyone who strays too far from group thoughts. Know this about groups before you get too involved and "locked in" to what "they" all think.

Now; when you begin to evolve to the extent that you are seeing things that are not yet proven but you *know* them to be so, remember that everything will change. As you go about your mission I wish you to remember to not lock into or on to anything. Pass through. Be flexible and move through areas of behavior. You are not here to get stuck to things so don't get too carried away with any discoveries and do not try to change everything along the way. You are the passenger now and you are just traveling through. Do not get stuck in rebuilding the train when your job is simply to ride the train. This is mostly a ride into heaven. I am moving you as gradually and yet as quickly as you can be moved. I am moving you up and out of your own dilemma and into freedom. You will become a free thinker, and this will allow you to see much that is not seen nor is it accepted by many – not yet anyway. Actually, there is always the possibility that everyone else has already seen and done it all, so they just came back here to help you go through it all. Anything is possible!

❧

You will begin to discover your true power when you begin to see how you are a light. You are not so much bones and skin and tissue as you are the energy that runs through you. You are the electric charge that you put out and you are the electric charge that you take in. So; where does this charge come from and how does this charge create for you? You are now at a point of discovery that will allow you to be total in your makeup. You are not one thing or another, you are all things. You are all beings and all energy. You are not black or white you are both. You are the duality that you have created. You may rise above your duality by asking to be shown the path to oneness. By asking to be shown your true existence in the higher realms you may leave duality behind.

You may also discover that you are the creator of all that has been your world. You will find that you no longer require a split of energy to create greater energy. No more cells splitting to create double or twice as much. You will begin to see how you are never in need of two ends or two sides of anything and you simply created it all to have a little excitement and contrast. Now that you are tired of excitement and contrast you wish to come back to oneness and leave the duality to everyone else.

So; as you begin this rise up out of duality you will begin to see how you no longer *require* struggle. Struggle will end when duality ends. Duality is the belief in one or the other. You need not choose sides, ever. You may simply say, "Well, I'm sure that whatever is meant to occur will occur." Does this thought frighten you? Does it frighten you to simply suggest that creation be allowed to unfold with complete trust that it will all work out somehow, or do you feel the need to roll up your sleeves and get involved and do something?

It does not matter you know? You can play this game any way you want and I do suggest that you allow everyone else to make their own free will choice. They may wish to simply observe and watch you run around like crazy trying to fix things and make things different. It is as though you believe that without you nothing would go right. You straighten things out and set them right. You are a great believer of right and of how things should or should not be. How would you like it if creation took over and said, "Take that, I'm going to flood you out because you are constantly judging every move and constantly planning new ways to change what is occurring. So I am now going to simply flood you out and get creation back." You have been flooded out before and it could occur again.

I think it is time to stop pushing at everyone and everything to do your will. After all, your will is only your ego at work. The will of God does not push and does not intimidate. The will of God does not require that everyone and everything pay homage to God. The will of God works with creation and flows with energy that is here. The will of God does not take one part of creation and make it the enemy simply because it is different. The will of God does not want to be pushy because there is no need to push, not ever. You will never hear God say, "Hurry up, we have to get this done. Time is short." That is simply nonsense. There is nothing but time and nothing must be done. Everything is just fine the way it is, it's all a misperception on your part. It is a maladjustment in your visual apparatus. You do not see clearly and so you are trying to fix all that you see when, in actuality, you need to adjust your vision. You will get it worked out and you will let go of your need for duality, and then you will see the whole picture instead of just one half of the side that you are accepting and calling whole.

As you learn to view from a wholeness of mind you will learn how easy it is to accept all parts of you. You will no longer section you into parts as you will no longer find it necessary to separate everything into categories of good and bad. You will allow everything to be and this will allow all parts of you to balance which will, in turn, allow your view of creation to balance. This distorted vision has too many problems and it is time to adjust to the truth and let go of the lie. You are not here to judge and to decide what is best and what is not. You are here to enjoy the adventure. It was originally meant to be a good time. You got too serious about what and how you create. Give it a rest. Let it be fun again. Stop judging it and allow it to be. Allow everything to be. Watch. Learn. Listen. You do not even know who you are so how can you say what everything else is?

***

As you begin to awaken, you will begin to see and feel many parts of you that you did not know existed. You will become aware of your own part in creation and you will become aware of how you have always taken part in creating your life. As you learn to discern between your own need to create and your own need for peace you will learn how to create from peace. You will learn how what you project out creates your life for you and what you hold in creates your life in you. You will begin to see how creation is not simply a projection it is also a stimuli. Creation moves and stimulates more of the same, and creation moves and creates more of what it is, and creation moves and you get more of what you already have. So, how do we slow down creation until we can get some positive influence running through it? I would say that the best way to slow down the creation is to slow down the creator. Get the creator to stop flying all over the place and his creation will begin to settle down too.

So, if you want calm and peace in your life slow down and feel calm and peace long enough to project it out into your creation. If you want love in your life begin to feel love long enough to project it out into your creation. If you want to be free, begin to feel free long enough to project it out into your creation. For some of you this will occur within days or weeks. For others it may take months. It depends on your level of intensity and your willpower and your ability to receive light and project light. It will, however, work for anyone. Try it and you will see.

Start small by focusing on one thing at a time. Focus on the feelings you wish to project. If it is a feeling or sense of kindness that you wish to receive then project kindness and watch for it to return. It may return from many places at once, or it may come in in small doses, or it may come back to you in a big kindness bolt. Either way it is all you creating what you want. Do not try to control who returns your kindness. That is not how creation works. Simply put it out there and watch to see how it returns.

When you begin to know how you can create such pleasures for yourself you will begin to see how you can change your entire life by changing what you project. This is a process by which you retrain the part of you who normally sends out the signals. Old signals from the past will read, "Come and get me because I don't like me." New signals from the future will read, "Let me rise above all of creation for I am God." You will "feel" this more when you are closer to it. For now you can send out signals that read, "I am light and I receive only light, therefore, all that I receive is light." This kind of fits it all into one package of all is goodness and I am one with the goodness of all.

As you begin to move and to accept more parts of you, you will begin to create new sources of energy that you had not previously tapped into. Some of these sources of energy are locked up in you and are trapped behind the pent up anger and frustration and rage. If you can unblock these areas you will create a new flow in you that was previously blocked. This will literally give you more of you to work with.

You may unblock these dense, stuck parts of you by releasing the energy that is sitting there. It may be as simple as a kick. Maybe you were small and really, really mad at your dad. You wanted to kick him so bad, but you could not. After all, he was about three times your size and he was authority, and we all have been taught to "be nice to someone who has power over you." So, you do not kick him, but you feel how good it would feel to kick and kick, and you may even visualize how you would do this. Now it is forty years later and you never got your kick out, but you have all the built up emotions that went into getting the kick out. Maybe you expelled some of these emotions by stomping out of the room or maybe you went and kicked at the cat, thankful that there was someone smaller than you for you to release your anger on.

So, you may have kicked the cat, but if your anger at your father was as great as your fear of his power, you have a block in you. Kicking a pillow and using it to release this energy, so that you may tap into these buried energy pockets in you, would be a very wise thing to do. Get it out and get it moving. Let the trapped resources in you begin to flow.

Everyone is angry and everyone wants to strike out. It is simply part of the release process. This is a much more collectively positive form of release than yelling at the kids, or withholding passion and romance, or many of your current acting-out patterns. You are all still dealing with power issues. Kick it out! Kick your pillows and get this energy moving. Get yourself worked up real good and beat a bed or hit a stuffed animal. It is not necessary to act out your human emotions on another human. Act out your problems in your private space. You are learning to deal with you, not with your spouse and not with your boss and not with your friend. "You" are the one that you are learning to deal with and to work things out with. "You" are the one that you must learn to like and then to love. "You" are the one that you must live inside of. We are taking you home to you. We are not taking you home to someone else's house. You get to live in you with all parts of you complete and whole.

You will begin to understand how you came to be confused as you begin to understand how you are gaining clarity. Most of what you know is surrounded by confusion and you do not really realize the full value of clarity. When you begin to shift your conscious view of reality you will be seeing with the eyes of love and clarity. Love is one of the most powerful vision clearing devices. As you learn how to handle love you will learn how to handle you. You are love and so it must follow that as you learn to handle the energy and the power that are you, you will be learning to handle love. Love is new to you in that you do not know that you are love and you have been hiding from love.

As you begin to learn more regarding the power of love, you will begin to see how you are not at all offensive and you no longer require the offensiveness of certain thought patterns. As you begin to release your defenses your offenses will automatically begin to crumble. You offend in a pattern. When you take on an offense position it is usually in order to defend your position. In becoming defensive you have actually crossed over into aggressive hostility. You overreact and you overplay your hand at every turn. You are becoming an attack machine without knowing that you are. When you begin to return to love you will no longer find it necessary to defend nor to attack. You are becoming all that you can be and all that you can be is love.

When you have become accustomed to the vibration of love, it will begin to grow and to be all that you have hoped for. Love is the ultimate. Love is the supreme.

Love is the limitlessness of your own true being. As you move into this limitlessness you will find that you are no longer in fear. Fear is limiting and fear is blind. Love sees and love knows. Love is all knowing and love does not require defensive nor offensive behaviors. You are becoming the purest part of you. You are becoming the part of you that is free to be and to express without repercussions. This will be a new you who does not punish you for free will choices. One of your greatest areas of confusion is in your choices. You decide to take action and then get upset with your own results. You are not only not within your own boundaries and limits; you actually have no boundaries or limits. So when you get upset at the result of a choice it is you not wishing to make a mistake. There is no right way and only you see mistakes.

As you make your choices I wish you to learn to ask only for God to guide you. Do not ask for God to do this or do that, as it is impossible for God to follow all of your instructions. This is due to the fact that so many parts of you are sending out so many different signals. As you begin to request guidance you will begin to look for new alternatives and, therefore, see new alternatives. In asking God to guide you, you are really asking love to guide you which is simply another way of trusting love and allowing yourself to be love. You are moving very quickly into a place that is accepting and will allow more of you to come to life.

As more of you comes to life you may see things you did not know about yourself and you may see things you do not like about yourself. This is a good way to find out why you do not like you and to let go of what you harbor inside of you. You may want to keep certain parts and release others. You are changing you and re-creating you as we go. You are becoming all that you are by merging or integrating all parts of you into "one." You are becoming whole and learning to look at and accept and love you. You are learning to be all that you are simply by allowing all that you are to come forward. It is good to look at you. It is good to know you. It is good to be you.

You will find that as you learn to go deeper and deeper into you, you are actually learning to bring more and more of you to the surface. This is a very good time. To expose your hidden parts to the light of day is very good. You will wish to know that you no longer need to suffer when you no longer have anything to hide from yourself. You are free when you can face yourself directly and without incrimination. You are free when you allow loving you to be an option. You are free when you allow being you to be an opportunity. Learn to love you and learn to live "in you" with great care and gratitude and love. You are being born and will rise up *in you*.

❧

*W*hen you begin to know your own intuition you will begin to understand how you can learn to be an intuitive being of light. You are no longer in a position to ignore your intuition and you are no longer in a position to be ignored. Once you begin to tune-in to your intuitive self you will be moving in a whole new direction. Intuition will begin to send you signals that will allow you to be totally free of guess work. You will begin to know you as never before and you will begin to react to new stimulus with a renewed sense of purpose. You will begin to react and act-out from a level of awareness instead of acting out of confusion. As you learn to intuit your situations you will begin to change how you handle certain situations. It is very important to learn to listen to your intuition, for it will cut through the layers of lies faster than a logical thought process. It is well known that your intuition is a good friend and it will lead you to discover some of your own dysfunctional behavior.

As you become more and more open to intuition you will allow it to grow. It has been lying dormant in you and now it is beginning to stretch and unfold in order to assist you in your rise up. As it unfolds for you, you will begin to know more and more what you do not want to keep and what you want. It is a simple process of paring down and trimming off the excess so that one might fly. With intuition one becomes quite free in one's choices and this process moves very quickly. As you learn to process your intuition you will learn to modify your response to any given situation. You will no longer feel as though you are being caught up in your own created web. This will begin to open an entire new area of you for you to explore. As you begin to explore your own intuitiveness you will be allowing it to expand into other areas and this will allow all parts of you to begin to expand in awareness.

You do not like to be intuitive because you do not like your feelings. When you know something intuitively you know with your feelings and it is not always easy for you to accept the truth. If someone is upset with you, and throwing negative energy at you, it is much easier to accept that you did something wrong and you must change your behavior. This is how you were taught as a child. The big people get upset, so you do better to try to keep the big people happy so they won't be grumpy and yell at you or hit you. Now you are an adult and you prefer to talk things out and everyone gets to lie and say, "No, I'm not angry," and you all lie about it and try to control your emotions. With intuition there is no lie. You must be honest with yourself as you are "feeling" the anger and, therefore, it is impossible to go into denial.

When you learn to use your intuition you will "feel" many energies very strongly and it will confuse you. You are not accustomed to accepting the fact that anger and resentment reign on this plane. You will not like to "open" to feeling. This is why you shut down your ability to feel. It is part of the protection mode that you set up. Protection is leaving now as we change from a need for protection to a need for trust in God. You will find that protection and defense are quickly slipping away and being replaced by light and intelligence. Ignorance has had a free reign for a very long time, but now it is time for a change or shift in consciousness. As you become aware of all of these shifts you will find it very uncomfortable at first. As you learn to integrate this new way of viewing reality it will become easier for you to shift the next time. Each step will become less and less of an effort. You will rise up more quickly as you begin to reclaim more and more parts of your own self.

You have many, many abilities that you are not aware that you have. As you learn to walk along your path to heaven you will learn to open you up to receive you back. You are recollecting the parts you sloughed off in order to become unconscious, and now, as you return to consciousness, you will recollect the parts that show you illumination. You are walking into the light and you are taking the dark with you. All is being transformed and changed and it is growing in strength. This is a process whose time has come and there is no stopping it once it gets going. It is in motion now and it is returning. All of it is returning. It is God returning to God. It is you returning to you. It is love returning and it is the light being born out of darkness.

❧

How is it that you no longer trust you and how is it that you no longer care for you? You are learning to be what you were never taught to be. You were never taught to be you. You were never taught to be you, and what is you was knocked out of you from the time that you were born. From the moment you arrived you knew what you wanted and what you did not want. You were then taught to do things for appearance sake and now your radar that automatically tells you what you want, or what you don't want, no longer works. Now you are left to depend on rules of propriety and rules of training and rules of your own for protection. You no longer know how to use your own intuition to know what you want or don't want. Often you make choices based on what you don't want instead of based on what you do want. You make choices based on how you think instead of how you feel. You have become very logical and not at all magical.

This will change. Everything regarding how you make your choices will change. You will become clear on what you want and how you want to be. You will become clear on how you will use your power, and when you have clarity you will no longer fear your power. As you learn to move into your own intuitive part of self you will begin to be confused by so many signals. You have never before received so much information and it will take some time to begin to balance and assimilate it all. You are no longer in a situation where you can simply say, "No, this is not right," because you have given up right and wrong. You will create confusion until you can learn to adjust. You will find that you are not only learning to adjust to your own intuitive design, you are also learning to be you once again. You really do know more than you are letting yourself know that you know. You are much brighter and much more aware than you let on.

So, as you begin to open your intuitive ability, I wish you to not judge yourself for feeling confused and uncertain. You will come into balance and you will learn to flow with your intuition and not be so afraid of it. It is simply a design system of analysis that allows you to determine what is really going on behind all the words. The words are being used to bend and control and get one's needs met. Intuition bypasses all those pretend words and gets down to what's really going on. You need not be so afraid to know what's really going on. After all, this is how you become aware and in-tune. You will find that you no longer wish to be unaware once you have gotten over your initial shock of being aware. You are moving into a new area now and this will allow you some stability in this new found shift in awareness.

For those of you who do not yet feel this shift, it is okay. Your turn will come. If you are not yet beginning to "tune in," you will as soon as the adjustments are made in you and as soon as you are ready. Nothing will happen for you until you are prepared. When you are ready you automatically draw the appropriate lessons to open you to higher understanding. You may not like your lessons when they are presented but you will learn to recognize their value in time. You will even learn to welcome them as you will soon begin to see the great benefit to you from such lessons. Now you are on a journey and this journey is to discover all of you. You carry power and energy as well as fear. It will all come together and it will all become balanced, and you will find your center and then you will ride your own energy into your bright new future.

You are creating a wave so that you might ride this wave. This wave is your own energy projected forth to create a ladder that spirals up and you then follow your own energy "up." You are matter. You are thought. Energy is matter and thought is energy. As energy moves it will follow thought that is projected, and that energy will create and manifest wherever you put it. Put it in a good place. Put it high and put it in light. You may create your heaven right here on earth or you may continue to live in the hell of confusion. It is up to you. You are creator, you are creation. You are also everything in between. So begin to look at "in between" and how it is all done. "Look at how you create it and you will know how to change it into something higher. You may simply change your mind about how you see it in most cases. Once you let go of seeing it as awful it becomes something other than awful. Your most uncomfortable situations can change for you at the least little shift in consciousness.

You are learning to be you and you are learning to experience all that you have created in order to know you better so that you might begin to see you for the very first time. You are growing with each new awareness and you are growing with each new insight. You are also shrinking as you grow. It is as though you were once composed of one thing and now you are decomposing and turning into something else. You are dying and being born anew and you do not need to kill your body to do so. You are transforming and you are now becoming more of what you are transforming into and less of what you once were. This is birth! God is being born into you by your free will choice. You invited God by your acceptance and now God (light) is becoming you. You are light!

≈❧≈

*W*hen first you begin to intuit your way around, you will find that you no longer feel the need to express your viewpoint. You will find that you are so taken with viewing every viewpoint that you no longer care to remain in just one point of view. As you continue to receive information from intuitive source, you will continue to add to your own growth and you will continue to expand. As this expansion begins to take over, you will begin to see how no one really makes a mistake and how no one really is off base or out of their own program. Everyone is really right where they are meant to be and everyone is assisting everyone else in their growth. After all, how would you grow without experience and how would you experience without the aid of those who teach you by assisting in this game of learning.

If you are not upset about something you will not get upset over anything that occurs. If you are upset about something you will easily get upset about anything that occurs. Your degree of upset already in you will determine how upset you might become in any given situation. So, get the upset out of you. You may use people or situations to trigger you or you may go ahead and trigger your own upset and get it out constructively. Beating up your bed is an excellent way to get it out. When you begin this type of therapy I want you to remember that you are human as well as God. You have a nervous system and you hold vibrations in. You require release of these vibrations so you will not explode. You could release by yelling and controlling others but it will bring other energies into play. If you release on a bed there are no repercussions unless, of course, you break your bed.

So, as you begin to trigger and release your pent-up energy in this constructive manner, you will be taking responsibility for your own garbage and no longer dumping it on the kids, or the dog, or your coworkers, or spouse, or, your favorite – "other relatives." You will begin to take full responsibility for you and for what is taking place inside of you. You will be responding to your own emotions without the added confusion of another's emotions. You will be learning to deal directly with you without any go-between. You will be in touch with you for one of the first times in your life. You will literally see how explosive you are and you will literally see how you can release your explosive behavior. This is a wonderful technique to teach children. It does not suppress anger, it allows it to flow forward and become constructive, and it also releases the child from his or her own fear of their own anger.

This is not a way of getting back at someone and it is not a way of letting someone get back at you. This stops the reaction to the response game. You no longer react to another; you simply carry your energy home and explode on your bed. It is not necessary to control others and tell others how it is. When you spend your energy trying to get others to see your reality you are in fear of other possible realities and this is why you are trying to control. When you can let go of your fear you can successfully live in *all* realities and not get too stuck to any single reality.

You will learn to release karma by no longer blaming or punishing another. In hitting a bed you are releasing without the use of another. This means you no longer require a partner to play this karmic game. This means cause and effect no longer is required. You are no longer bound to hurt another because he or she hurt you in another life. You are no longer responding to past programming and you are now creating a whole new role for yourself. This is a role that is self-contained and free of emotional conflict. You simply "get it all out" and move on to the next level. You begin to release all the debris that is blocking you, and you no longer feel you owe another soul for your release from your personal hell or energy blocks. You only owe you, which is right where you want to be.

You are the creator and you are the creation. You are moving you up the ladder to love and light and insight, and you will have a whole new perspective on all of creation. You will have a view that is so grand that you will be surprised at the greatness of it all.

As you begin to move forward in your spiral upward you will wish to remain calm as you view your new reality. After all, it is your reality and if you shout how you have arrived you will only create waves of shock and energy that will not be understood by those who are seeing their own view. It is as though you are looking into a viewfinder and each individual is focused on his or her own view. Do not yell and scream, simply watch. Do not project your view onto another or you might give your view away (literally) and you will be lost and wondering how you lost it. Stay calm and know that you are rising up and simply seeing what is on the rise. The view can be quite spectacular and you will bump into others who are seeing your same view. This will happen as you are ready and it will allow you to share your gifts and to share your feelings.

This is not a time for becoming hung up on things. It is not a time to get all involved in group activities so that you might feel connected to others. I know that you think of "one" as all of you hooked together and working together, but you are mistaken in your diagnosis of the situation. Mostly you need to unhook, and let go of groups and organizations, in order to find out who you are and how you work. Within a group structure it is too easy to follow the leaders and there are always leaders in groups. The strong always come forward and lead while the weak try to follow their example. Outside of a group you are free to follow your own intuitive source. You are not being led around by the nose, but you are showing yourself your own way which may be totally opposite of what the group *thinks*. Group consciousness holds you to it and slows you down. Go off on your own. Think for yourself. Do not be programmed to follow the ways or patterns of a group. You are just creating more programming for yourself to clear at another time.

Set yourself free of constructed ways. Do not follow rules to get to heaven. Be you. Live in you. Take responsibility for you and do not follow like a pack of sheep. Religion has kept you held in a single position and now many groups are rising up to say, "No, follow our way. Your way won't get you there." Do not follow anyone or any group. Follow only your guidance from inside of you. You will find it in your heart. Follow your heart and you will find yourself at home with you, and not out paying homage to a group that you admire. Stay home and pay "attention" to you, for you have your own path to walk and "attention" is energy. You are giving the majority of you away to everyone else. Keep you for you. Pay very close "attention" to you and you will be validating you instead of validating everyone else.

⚜

As you begin to see how you are changing, you will begin to feel uncomfortable and out of sorts. You will no longer know who you are and you will become a little uncertain. This is due, in part, to the fact that you are letting go of old stubborn ways and you are becoming new and flexible. With this new flexibility will come new ways of dealing with many situations. As with anything, you have a certain amount of un-sureness when you begin to work in new areas. This un-sureness is a very good thing. It is much better to be unsure of yourself than it is to be so stuck that you know it all. You are much better off being insecure and floating than you are when you are stuck in a certain position, or idea, or stance and no one can get into your space to change your mind or your stubborn ways. You are much better when you are flexible and it is much healthier for you.

As you begin to know how it feels to no longer hang on to one position or another position, you will begin to feel a little frustrated as you see all of your possibilities. Do not give up hope. Just because there are so many possibilities does not mean that it is not important to hope for higher evolution and a clearer point of view. Once you see how all possibilities are available to you, you will see how very many choices you always have. Most of you think that you must do something this way or that way and do not realize that you are actually dealing with many, many ways of doing anything at any time. It does not matter what choice you make when you come from love. Once you have changed to love, you will never find one choice better than another. All choices become valid and nothing is invalidated. As you learn to view every possibility as a free will choice, you will begin to see how everything comes to you and you simply say, "Yes please" or "No thank you." You need never explain, you need never feel pressured regarding your choice.

As you begin to receive, you will begin to see how you are creating for you by the choices you are making. At this time certain parts of you are stubborn and unable to say, "Yes please" because they have been stuck in, "No, we cannot let anyone or anything get the best of us" for so long. You have parts of you, who have protected you by pushing life away from you for so long, that if anyone gets too close they may get burned by this overzealous part of you. This part and others like it are changing as you grow in awareness. You are educating all parts of you simply by becoming "aware." You are learning to grow and to evolve as you do so. Some parts of you will have an easier time than other parts. You must give yourself time to adjust, or you will simply give up and slip back into your old ways of stubbornness and being stuck. Be flexible with you. Be gentle with you. Be nice to you. Be loving to you.

As you learn to distinguish between where you are going and where you have been you will find it very interesting. You will see how you are moving forward and yet you do not seem to be making headway. You seem only to be moving and this is good. You are shifting up and it requires movement. Get your emotions moving and your mind moving and your energy shifting. You will find this all a very good thing when you can come to a place where you can look back on it with clarity. You will see how you are being moved and how you are literally traveling at a certain velocity and speeding up all the while. This speed does not necessarily have to do with movement forward in life which is how you are accustomed to judging everything. Movement forward gives you a feeling of getting somewhere. This is more like movement "within" and change "within," and you know you are different but it doesn't seem to show so much in your everyday life.

You are not moving ahead in leaps and bounds. What you are doing is spinning and vibrating at such a speed that you are beginning to go "up" instead of forward. You are experiencing no movement forward and yet so much is going on within you. You are beginning to move up out of positionality, out of your stuck position. You are moving up into a perspective that will allow you freedom from one or the other and give you *all*. You want "all" because "all" is what you actually are. You are not limited you are total.

As you begin to experience this rise above duality you may begin to focus on more and more duality. Sometimes what you are leaving is actually rising up in you to leave. Sometimes it is not so much you moving out of a stuck position as it is a stuck position moving out of you. So, as you begin to leave your position in duality it will begin to grow as it goes. It will become strong and you will want to judge things more than ever. Try to flow and stay calm. Try to allow it all to be just a process and don't get overwhelmed by it.

This too shall pass. You will know how to handle your emotions and you will do very well because you are already vibrating at a new level just from all the information you have been processing. You are going up and this is a new direction for you. You will adjust and you will be okay. Continue to release and to stay calm. You are working on levels within you that have not been addressed in a very long time. Some parts of you are in total disarray while other parts have been packed and ready to go for a long time. It is like moving from one location to another, and sorting out what you want to keep and take to the new place and what you no longer need.

You have a great deal of understanding yet to achieve but you are moving ahead without understanding. You are moving into trust which has little to do with logic and understanding. Trust feels very different and it creates differently than logical understanding. You are in a whole new world when you enter the world of trust. Welcome!

❦

You will begin to discover how you no longer believe in the difference between right and wrong. When you discover this you will be feeling very disquieted and quite unbalanced. Your balance for so long has been to be lopsided and it will require a huge shift in your awareness to bring you into balance. Most of you do not realize that you are who you are. You are so afraid of being different from others that you do not realize how to be happy to be different from others. As you begin to understand the workings that make you up you will begin to realize how it is good to break away from what is considered normal.

You are moving farther away from what is considered normal and closer to what is not normal. What is not normal is God. Rarely do you hear of someone who works for God and talks with God and is learning to allow God to take over. God is not a normal part of your discussions. Religion maybe, but God is rarely on your mind. When you begin to focus on God you will receive God. God is part of you, and you need only begin to focus on how God is in you to begin to open you up to his presence.

Now; you all know that God is not a "he." God "is." You have no problem with the use of certain words used to describe your world because you know that words are just words. So, as you begin to discover this God that "is" in you, you may feel it as anything that is most appealing to you. You may feel it as energy, or consciousness, or heat, or light, or sound, or boy, or girl, or nothing, or everything. For each of you "this divine presence" will be significant in its own way and will be very personal. If such a presence is personal to each individual it is best to keep it personal and not get into feeble minded discussions about what God is. "God is." Let that be it.

You need not discuss the variety of ways you meet God and you need not feel pulled to discuss how you are on your path to ascension. Sometimes, it is more to your advantage to be God rather than discuss the fact that you are. You are moving into a time that, for you, will be just such a time. It is not necessary to compete for God for he belongs to everyone. You all have this competition thing and this has created all the religions and all the attitudes that say, "I have the true God, yours is false." In reality, it is all make believe and none of you know the truth.

You will find that as you allow each individual to embrace his or her own God, you are allowing each individual to be their own God. You will also find that in a time of imbalance you will do well to allow yourself to heal and balance before you try to convince others that you know anything. Your balance is off and so are you. At times you are way off base and have no center to speak from. So, rather than speaking now and creating misinformation and messes to clean up later it is best to be you and stay quiet and calm.

To be you, you do not necessarily have to express verbally to everyone who you are, or more aptly put, who you think you are. Let it all go. Do not try to impress others with your brilliance. Your brilliance has nothing to do with how you are God. You're impressing others has little to do with being God. Presenting a false façade for others to see is simply a way to disguise yourself, to make you feel better about who you are because you do not believe you are good enough as you. So, drop the façade and be you. You will have a more honest view of yourself and you will draw those to you who are more honest.

As you learn to drop the façade and be who you are you will find it difficult to remember that you are God. Part of you believes you are the farthest thing from God when, in actuality, you are in God and God is in you. So, when this part of you, who believes he is very low on the scale of love, begins to come to the surface he will want to brag to make himself feel better or he will want to put others down to make himself feel better. This is the part of you who is most dark and most unloved. He will come to the surface kicking and screaming for love, and you will be made to love him or leave him behind. He is the part of you that you most judge and he is the part of you who will be most apparently in pain.

You will be allowed to view this part of you, and to embrace this part of you and make him part of the whole by accepting him and no longer judging him or, better put, no longer judging you for being him. He is your darkness and your fear and he will very much need love and understanding, and criticism will kill him. He will not handle criticism well, and he will be most defensive and he may attack believing he is being attacked. He has no balance and never has. He is here to learn to become balanced and to live in the light. He does not know how to love and does not know how to accept love. You must now become him in order to own him. If you own him you may transform him. If you disown him he remains a parallel you who bumps into you periodically to gain attention. You will not be rid of him by simply disowning him. You will, however, transform him by owning him.

He is your unhealed heart. He is the part of you that is lowest in esteem. He is a part of you who never had a chance because he came from the wrong side of the tracks. He is dark and dark is considered bad, wrong, dangerous. He never got to express his truth and he never got to be. He has been pushed down by religion and suffocated by you. He is angry and unhappy and miserable, and if he continues to be pushed down "in" you, he will continue to push out his anger and miserableness into your world and your life.

I suggest that you get to know this part of you and that you allow this part of you to "be." In allowing him to be you will be completing the cycle of who you are. There are big parts of you that you do not allow to be. Now is the time to allow everyone and everything to be.

꧁꧂

*A*s you begin to grow and to recognize your potential for greater growth, you will begin to see an even greater shift in your awareness. You will begin to see how you are creating everything as you go and, therefore, you can change what you create simply by being aware of it. It is not so much that you must watch every little move you make as it is that you must be aware that what you do has an effect on your life. How you think and how you see your world can directly affect the changes that take place in your world. You are under no obligation to think a certain way or be a certain way. It will help you if you know what thought can do and what belief "held in" you can do. It creates electricity that must go somewhere. It creates currents that must be discharged, or meltdown or buildup will occur.

Most of you are in excess energy buildup which eventually causes a meltdown and running off of all your energy. You may get sick a little here or there or you may have emotional explosions a little here or there. Either way it is built-up, pent-up charge. It is trying to go somewhere. It was taken in and held in and not released. It is trauma and pain that were never expressed. You didn't cry because you were told big boys and girls don't cry. Now it is still in you and you must create something big enough to make you cry. Once in awhile a movie or good novel will make you cry and you can release some of this built-up charge. It will eventually turn into rage and then depression. First you will find yourself getting overly upset, and then you will close off that part of you, and your rage will slide further down the tunnel of denial and it will eventually become depression. Then your doctor will call it stress depression and give you a pill to take to shut that part of you off.

You continue to shut off parts of you until there is no you left in you and you are in total and complete denial, and then you die from sheer exhaustion and call it aging or old age. You do not need to shut you down and let you die. Continue to be in you. Let your emotions move and begin to express who you are. Who you are is a hurt or confused little person. Let your emotions begin to move out of you by crying or hitting your bed. Begin this shift in emotional awareness. Your emotions are blocked to the extent that you use only your anger and self-righteousness. You use little else and you are way out of balance.

Open to crying. Be a crybaby and allow the tears to cleanse away the built-up charge. It does not matter how you make yourself cry. It will work for you whether it is emotional pain, or sadness, or physical hurt. I suggest you allow yourself to cry in private to allow yourself the space you require to heal and balance your emotions. If you tell everyone how you are crying to discharge yourself you only "involve" them and it becomes a drama instead of a release. Leave the drama out for awhile. You have way too much drama in your life now. Begin to see how you can balance your own emotional body without shutting it up with medication. Allow all parts of you to speak to you in their own way. As you begin to do this you will be opening more of you up to you.

You have closed off so many parts of you by becoming an adult that it is time to reopen some of what you have shut away. This is a return to life for these parts. This is the opposite of death and it will allow you to grow instead of wilt. It will allow you to return to health and leave death and illness behind. You will be unlocking you and it will be huge parts of you that you unlock and allow to take part in your life. You will be taking on more of you which reverses the process that you have been in. Your way is to shut down. God's way is to open up. So, you will open and receive you and, as you open and receive you, you will be receiving God.

You cannot lose here. You are in a win/win situation and this entire process is opposite of what you are now taught. Your current belief is that you get old and die. I am now telling you that, as you grow in age, you will begin to truly be you for the first time since birth. You had it then and you knew it then, but you could not rationally use this information. Once your rational mind was trained, it was trained to know opposite information. You can only be what you were trained to be. I am now telling you that you can untrain and unlearn and see it all differently. As you do you will evolve into whatever your new belief is. What do you currently "hold in" you? What are you becoming? Who are you and how did you get to be this you? You have no problem saying, "Well, that's just who I am," but who taught you to be who you are and is it really who you are?

❧❦❧

*W*e will begin to see great changes in body, mind and spirit. This is a time of great change and it will last for many of your years. Some will wake sooner than others and some have an easier time of it than others. You are each individual and yet part of the whole. You are each growing and expanding in order to play your part. As you learn to uncover your true identity you will be learning to know who you are and how you are programmed. In knowing how you are programmed you may deprogram and change everything about your current life. You may literally transform into another life form simply by knowing you and changing what you know. You have the ability to do so and you have the ability to be all that is available to you. This takes a little doing but it is very possible for each of you.

The mind will lead you through your thoughts so do not judge the mental process that will allow you to figure things out. The soul will lead you through yourself and will allow you to experience the past from a new perspective. And the body, who stores it all, will ache and desire movement and it all begins to shift and change. Be kind with your body. Be gentle with all of you. Do not push and bully you. Love you and know that you are actually working as one unit to restore all of you as whole and complete. All parts will have problems as you begin to change. The soul will want out as it is easier to fly than to stay grounded in the pain that must move up and out. The mind will want it all to stop. The processing of old programs becomes too much and the mind will scream for relief and your body will ache from certain areas of release. As the old programs come to the surface, and the anger and rage are felt by your cells, you may have soreness or stiffness, and body massage will help during this part of your process.

This is the Second Coming. It is the coming of you (God) into you. It is the birth of God into matter. It is the reuniting of Father/Mother God. Negative energy and positive energy are melding into one cell. Instead of cells dividing to create more, cells are reuniting to create wholeness. No more good or bad. Everything will be good. No more right or wrong, everything will be right. You will no longer haggle over words because it will no longer matter. Competition will slip away. The veil of darkness will flutter to the ground as if it never was. It is not so much the bringing together of light and dark as it is the emergence of light. After all, darkness is only a shadow caused by light reflecting off of only part of something. When light hits everything at once there is no room for shadow.

As you learn to rise up and to appreciate your own ascension you will begin to feel so good about being you. You will relish the fact that you are who you are. You will no longer wish for what is not part of you, as you will be so gloriously happy in being you that you could not imagine having more. It will be like having a birthday party and the gifts just keep coming and coming and coming, and you do not know how you can possibly hold all of these beautiful gifts at one time. It will be a truly glorious time for you and you will have walked into your own on your own two feet. You will have done this by your own processing of information and deprogramming and training your own self. You and God trusting each other enough to allow you and God to merge into oneness: God brought down into creation to walk among you and in you as part of you.

You are no longer "human" and "thought process" once you reach this point. You become more "spirit" and less human and you become more "God" and less mind. You will find that you are "all that is" and you can move in this pattern for eternity. You can develop practices and patterns that will assist you in moving further into God until you are literally at the center of God and no longer at the fringe trying to get closer in. You will begin to discover that God is vast and you are part of that vastness. You may *move* within God as God allows movement, and God is drawing in at this time. This is a very good time and you are reaching out now and touching God. You are moving into position to be able to come to full recognition and full consciousness. God is here!

You will find that you no longer require so much help from outside once you begin to feel God within you. He will lead and guide you from within and he will allow you the time you require to adjust to all of your changes. You are moving into God and God is merging with you.

We will discuss this further in our next book titled *I Touched God*. Until then I wish you well and I wish you love.

God

God's Pen

I first heard the voice of God in 1988. I was sitting in my back yard reading a book when this big booming voice interrupted with, "I am God and I will not come to you by any other name." I felt like the voice was everywhere – inside of me as well as in the sky around me. I was so frightened that I ran in my bedroom to hide.

This was not the first time that I heard voices. I had been communicating with my own spirit guide or soul for about a year. I guess my depth of fear regarding God, and all that he represented to me at the time, was just too much.

I spent two days trying to avoid the voice of God, which was patiently waiting for me to respond. By the second day I was exhausted from lack of sleep and decided to give in and talk with him. This turned out to be the greatest gift and best decision of my life.

The first book, *God Spoke through Me to Tell You to Speak to Him*, shows my evolution from communicating with my soul to communicating with the Big Guy. It took a couple years for me to be comfortable communicating with God. My fear of a punishing God was big! That has most definitely changed and I now think of God as my partner and best friend.

In the beginning the voice of God would wake me in the middle of the night and tell me it was time to write. He said I had promised to do this work (I assumed he was talking about the soul/spirit me). I would drag myself up to a sitting position and watch in amazement as my hand flew across the page, while I tried to keep up by reading what was being written.

It was always so much fun to wake up the next morning and grab my notebook to see what God had written during the night. After some time the voice stopped waking me and I became comfortable picking up my pen and writing for God first thing in the morning. I think in the beginning I had to be awakened while still semi-conscious from sleep so I wouldn't object too much to the information that was being channeled through me.

As I grew less and less afraid (and more trusting) of God, he was able to communicate greater information. Some of the information is quit controversial, but I felt it important to just let it be and not censor it. I present the writings here to you as they were given to me. I have edited a little (mostly the more personal information regarding myself) and I have used a pen name for privacy reasons. I asked God for a good pen name and he guided me to Liane which (I was told) in Hebrew means "God has answered."

At one point I became a little concerned about my sanity in all this, so I went to a hypnotherapist to find out what I was doing. Under hypnosis I saw this incredibly huge beam of light with a voice coming from within it. It was a giant "loving light" and felt so comforting and kind. It felt like that's where I came from. After that I stopped worrying about my sanity. If this is crazy, I think it's a very good kind of crazy to be….

In loving light, Liane

Loving Light Books

Available at:
Loving Light Books: www.lovinglightbooks.com
Amazon: www.amazon.com
Barnes & Noble: www.barnesandnoble.com

Also Available on Request at Local Bookstores